MASSEY H. SHEPHERD, JR. is Professor
of Liturgics, Church Divinity School of the
Pacific, Berkeley, California. He is also the
author of *The Oxford American Prayer Book
Commentary* and *The Reform of Liturgical
Worship,* and he is the editor of *The Eucharist and Liturgical Renewal* and *The Liturgical Renewal of the Church.*

WORSHIP IN SCRIPTURE AND TRADITION

WORSHIP IN SCRIPTURE AND TRADITION

Essays by Members of
the Theological Commission on Worship
(North American Section) of the Commission on
Faith and Order of the World Council of Churches

EDITED BY
MASSEY H. SHEPHERD, JR.

NEW YORK   OXFORD UNIVERSITY PRESS   1963

Copyright © 1963 by Oxford University Press, Inc.
Library of Congress Catalogue Card Number: 63-19947
Printed in the United States of America

Editor's Preface

Our essays in this volume are a portion of the studies prepared during the years 1954 through 1962 by members of the North American Theological Commission on Worship of Faith and Order. Our discussions and researches centered in the theological, cultural, and social forces that have shaped the patterns of worship in the varied traditions of our American Churches. We have sought to lay bare the reasons why our common allegiance of faith has been divided by our differing understandings of Christian worship.

Inevitably we were driven to study anew the fundamental sources that all of us claim as the wellspring of our several traditions — the teaching of the Bible, and the practice of the New Testament and early Catholic Church. Our large agreements about the meaning of this heritage were very much tempered by our recognition of how far the worship of so many of

our Churches, regardless of their denominational af-
filiation, fails to reveal either the depths or the heights
of Biblical revelation and apostolic truth.

In our essays we have endeavored to avoid superficial and arid polemic, and to set forth constructive
reassessments of what we believe to be of primary importance for the renewal of worship in our Churches
and for their reunion in the one Body of Christ according to God's will. Though we have often differed in matters of detail, we have sensed in our common exchanges such basic concord and sympathy in
the larger issues, that no attempt has been sought or
made to rewrite our papers according to any "mind of
the committee." The essays remain basically in the
form in which they were initially presented and re-
viewed, with only such slight revisions as were needed
for clarification. Each essayist speaks for himself, from
his own mind and conscience. Yet each has the satis-
faction of support and encouragement from his col-
leagues.

To our regret, two papers submitted by members
of the commission on themes closely related to the
subjects expounded in this volume could not be included because of prior commitments for publication.
One, by Professor Markus Barth of the University of
Chicago, "Was Christ's Death a Sacrifice?" has been

published as Occasional Paper No. 9 of the *Scottish Journal of Theology* (Oliver and Boyd, 1961). The other, by Professor J. Philip Hyatt of Vanderbilt University, on "The Prophetic Criticism of Israelite Worship," will be published in the near future as the Goldensen Lecture at Hebrew Union College. Of the papers here included, only one has been previously printed — that of the editor on "The Origin of the Church's Liturgy," which appeared in the July 1962 issue of *Studia Liturgica*. We are grateful to the editor of this newly founded "International Ecumenical Quarterly for Liturgical Research and Renewal," Pastor Wiebe Vos, for his kind and ready consent to republish it here. The essays of Professors Herzog and Schmemann were completed too late for a face-to-face discussion by the commission as a whole. We are fortunate in being able to give them this wider circulation.

These papers in no way constitute an official report of our commission; such report has been published through the agency of the Secretariat of the Commission on Faith and Order of the World Council of Churches.

To the several contributors to this symposium, the editor expresses his sincere gratitude for their ready co-operation and unfailing help, and to our chairman

— Professor Joseph A. Sittler of the University of Chicago — we are all indebted not only for his introductory essay but for all his stimulating guidance and patient forbearance of us during the years of our association.

Berkeley, California   M. H. S., Jr.
July 1963

Contents

ix

WORSHIP IN SCRIPTURE
AND TRADITION

Introduction

The editor of this volume has asked me to write an introduction in which the specific concern of each contribution might be related to the steady and growing attention to worship that exists in the work of the ecumenical movement.

While, to be sure, the effort of the World Council of Churches to bring us into such conversation as might advance all toward the unity of Christ's Church is not the source of the present, fresh attention to worship, the encounters made possible by the Council have surely been an occasion for such attention. Very early in the discussions of the Faith and Order of the Churches it became clear that doctrine and order were by no means the only factors that have contributed to estrangement among the Churches. Ways of worship have not only evolved in organic relation to theological starting points, methods and traditions — they have also served to solidify, enclose, and even isolate those theological positions from any engagement with others. Hence it was resolved, at the Third World Conference on Faith and Order at Lund, Sweden, in 1951, to appoint a commission on worship, to give continuing attention to this central gift and activity of the Christian community.

The commission thus appointed was divided into three sections — East Asia, Europe, and North America. While each section has profited by the papers produced by the others, a large measure of independence characterizes their statement of the problem, their chosen fields of inquiry, and their final reports.

In this brief preparatory essay I shall attempt to designate several central meanings and energies of corporate Christian worship. Not all such are enumerated, but no exhaustive specification could, in my judgment, ignore the following:

I

Worship is recollection and summary of the power from God that enables the Church. Christian worship is not unspecified and generalized adoration; it is absolutely specific and clearly pointed. Here is a community; and it is here and is a community because it acknowledges that something happened — and that from God — before the community happened. This revelation, action, endowment, liberation, imperative is the given substance of that assembly which is here as a body that participates in these bestowals. And central, therefore, and informing all Christian worship, from the most improvised to the most traditional, is this effort, conscious or uncalculated, to affirm that what has happened and continues to happen from God is the engendering force that grounds the present happening.

The community, for instance, sings, or speaks, or ejaculates the term *Glory*. This utterance may be found in the magnificent measures of Tallis or Gibbons or Merbecke or Bach or Glinka, or according to the shapes of Gregorian psalm-tone. Or it may break out to punctuate the discourse of the back-country preacher.

But it occurs. And there has never been and is not now a corporate action of Christian worship in which it does not occur. The term *Glory* when used in worship is a recollecting term in which is acknowledged that there has taken place an action not of men's possible accomplishment, a revelation not of men's conceiving, an illumination not of men's lighting, and a liberation not of men's contriving. A world is made available whose source, scope, meaning, and immeasurable peace find in the word *Glory* the amplest and deepest acknowledging sound. This word when used in worship is a repetition-from-below of the term used in Scripture to specify the presence and power of God. In Creation, at Sinai, at Bethlehem, at Calvary, on Easter morning, and at the Ascension, the *Glory* is the comprehensive term; and all Christian worship is a recollection, an attestation, a celebration, a thanksgiving — an acknowledgment that our being here in this particular situation is incomprehensible apart from the presence and power of the Glory.

I I

Worship is cultic recovery of the plenitude of the voice of the Christian community.

The deeds of God in his trinitarian reality as Creator, Redeemer, and Sanctifier, and the substance of men's response to these in life and word, have occurred in time and space. But these deeds and these responses, forming the Christian community, while actualized in concrete, particular times and places, are not exhausted in such actualizations. The reality of God's gracious relation of himself to men, that is to say, becomes concrete in the acknowledgment that is created and evoked by the Spirit among specific people in particular places and actual church traditions. But it is in the nature of all things historical that men are tempted to define the power by the place of its concretization for them; that they are tempted to restrict the Presence to the conditions within which it addressed *them;* that they are tempted to sing the song of adoration according to the score by which the Glory broke into and cracked open their lives.

The Glory creates voices to respond to it; and these voices, in word and liturgical form, are thickly real and substantial in virtue of the particular cultural possibilities available for use. The worshipping life of the Christian ages would be poor if it did not possess the rich variety of such particular responses: the stately movement and gesture of the Orthodox rites, the transmutation into a powerful and theologically instructive hymnody of the English church-song, the probing and pathos and judgment of the German chorale.

But this gathering up from the cultural vitality of a certain place and people in-order-to praise, and the very variety and multiple accents of it, is a kind of pedagogy for the whole Christian community. For the "natural" ways of each people and place are reminded, by their knowledge and sharing of the others, that the Glory has a plenitude never to be enclosed within any people, place, or time.

III

Worship is theologically necessary — for it is the Church's confession that the ways of knowing are many and complex.

In Père Jean Daniélou's *God and the Way of Knowing* (Meridian Books, 1957) there is an elaboration of six of the ways by which men have been and are brought to the knowledge of God. This exposition is a valuable warning that no single form of theological speech is completely adequate to the huge variety of the human.

Man is multiphasic; and worship is the multiphasic witness of the Church to the power and the presence of God. It has drama, and thereby relates the moving *history* of God's grace to the moving historical needs of men. It has intellectuality in virtue of its affirmations, and, by fusing its affirmations with episodes related in Gospel and Epistle, it invites the mind to entertain a mode of truth that transcends the propositional. It has an astounding spectrum of emotionally authentic elements, and thereby addresses the pathos and delight of man's immediate awareness of his own existence in the world and among his fellows.

Any effort to account for the movement toward the renewal of liturgical life in our day which does not relate this movement to the impoverishment of the human that empirical science has produced will result in superficial judgments. Or worse: it will attempt to use this longing for fullness that grounds the movement to lubricate temperamental dispositions toward ceremonial scrupulosity, ritual prissiness, or the multitude of marginal ritual cosmetics that continue to reduce to banality a profound need of men.

The essays that follow represent the sober efforts of several men, each working out of his area of special competence, to bring light to the nature and problem and promise of Christian worship.

ROBERT E. CUSHMAN

Worship as Acknowledgment

I THE ROOTS OF WORSHIP

To speak authentically of worship is always to point
beyond man to the Mystery overarching his existence.
It is also to say something important concerning man.
It is to speak of something that properly does not per-
tain to the birds of the heaven, to the beasts, or to
the lilies of the field. Devoid of option and, therefore,
the anxiety of ambivalence, these creatures unresist-
ingly glorify their Maker in the unfolding of the po-
tentialities of their being. Only to man is reserved the
option and the freedom to resist the *conatus* of his
being by centering his existence in his own will to
self-affirmation and so to incur the gnawing anxiety,
the guilt of unacknowledged dependency.[1] In his
dreadful freedom, which is also his possible glory, man
daily confronts and makes his decision. It is a choice
between apparent fulfillment through self-assertion or
true fulfillment through acknowledgment of responsible dependency.

9

To speak of worship, then, is to speak of the uniquely human alternative to self-affirmation. It is, to use a phrase of Jonathan Edwards, "consent to Being." But, unlike the "consent" of the other creatures, worship is man's witting and wholly voluntary consent. Without it man's self-consciousness tends toward alienation from Being and the anxiety of self-imposed privacy. Worship is the overcoming of alienation and the establishment of community through consent to Being, first to the Being of God, and, through Him, consent to the being and inherent worth of the creatures.

With some ages and cultures, the integral place accorded to worship was testimony that the whole of man's story is not exhausted in an account of his external relations. It implied that the whole of man's business is not with "the world" but with reality that does not lie-to-hand and is not manageable but must, nevertheless, be reckoned with. In such a context, worship is the implied acknowledgment that, however strenuously man shapes his ends, he is, nevertheless, often mysteriously overruled. Call it *moira*, fate, or *nemesis*, or call it *logos*, man is sensible of a destiny not of his own shaping and an order not of his own ordering. Worship signifies his acknowledgment that the apparent configuration of things and events, rather than being the powers with which he deals, are manifestations of deeper lying powers or of a Power of decisive moment with which he ultimately deals.

But the powers, or Power, that are half-hidden and half-revealed in the appearances inspire awe and are shrouded in sublimity and evoke both reverence and homage. This acknowledgment, this consent to Being, not simply to beings, inaugurates and sustains new dimensions of experience. On the one hand, it is the dimension of the *noumenous* in so far as all that is immediately given is apprehended as emerging from and dissolving again in mystery worthy of reverence. But it is also the dimension of responsibility, that is, responsibility for something and to something quite other than all that is entailed in man's aboriginal impulse to manage and utilize the immediate appearances in the attainment of sensuous satisfactions. It is responsibility to a good that does not yet appear and to truth that, only half disclosed, remains to be revealed. Herewith is invoked a sense of loyalty to imperatives whose credentials, still bafflingly obscure, are not thereby less commanding. And herewith the hitherto unchallenged and impulsive bent to manage and control the environment for immediate ends is confronted by an imperious counter-claim that serves notice of its authority and lays man under obligation.

Man's consent to the higher sovereignty, though halting and partial, is worship or nascent worship. Its onset is a sign, *semeion*, of man's dawning awareness of a new irrevocable and basic ambiguity within his existence as *humanum*. As a responsible being, he has acquired a trans-phenomenal reference, that is, by accepting, however partially, answerability to the good that does not yet appear and the truth that is yet to be revealed. For him, time (*chronos*) is no longer the endurance of fulfillment as with the creatures. Time is the interval between his election and the fulfillment of his vocation. It becomes *kairos*, the time for decision. Under claim, he is laid hold of, acquires subjectivity, and so becomes a person. Thenceforth his relations to Being are personal relations. In him, history has supervened upon mere nature, *kairos* upon *chronos*, self-consciousness upon consciousness, conscience upon science.

Worship is the matrix of this transformation. Man may still view himself as of the earth, earthy, but his conversation is somehow in heaven. He can withhold conversation, he can cease to converse; that is always the option of his freedom, but he cannot wholly stifle the presentiment that he has been addressed and that his chief business is to make responsible answers. If he attenuates conversation, if his consent to Being grows to be halting and is withheld, if worship goes cold within him, then he is hung in anxious suspense between the two resident impulses of his personal existence and lives in unresolved inner contrariety, as Socrates described the matter to Callicles.[2] He may continue to traduce and denature his conferred hu-

manity, his responsible personhood, by contenting himself with the management and utilization of the things
that lie to hand. Eventually he may become a casual,
even a "serene secularist." [3] This is the alternate option
open to man's freedom; the other is the fulfillment of
worship.

Worship, as consent to Being, defines the way in
which man's distinctive nature as personal being is fulfilled. For, in worship, according to Biblical language,
man hears, heeds, and consents to the divine will and
election. On the one hand, election is a summons to
action and service; on the other and more fundamentally, it is a summons to enter into a relation best
described by the words "I will be their God, and they
shall be my people" (Jer. 31:33). Mature worship is
acceptance of election which, in turn, constitutes man's
fulfillment of being, that is, of being-in-community —
fundamentally with God and, derivatively, with men.
Worship is responsible existence in which man lives
now under the rule of God while yet God's Kingdom
remains fully to be revealed. Worship is therefore inherently eschatological in perspective. But true worship is also eschatological existence without constraint,
since it is the glad and eager acknowledgment of the
claims of the Kingdom. It serves the Lord with fear
and yet rejoices with trembling (Ps. 2:11). It cries,
"O God, Thou art my God; early will I seek Thee:
my soul thirsteth for Thee . . ." (Ps. 63:1). The

language of worship is prayer; it is a sign of man's apprehension that he stands in the higher Presence and must speak appropriately.

II   THE MODERN ALTERNATIVE TO WORSHIP

Today it must be admitted that worship has dwindling significance for hosts of our contemporaries, even in the churches. For the casual and for the "serene secularist," worship is a word that has dwindling power to impart meaning or to excite interest. Insofar as meaning survives at all, it arouses otiose recollections of archaic churchly usages from which, by some strange alchemy, relevance to actual life has gradually been evacuated. In an age when, it would seem, more respectful heed was given to the affirmation of *The Shorter Catechism*, "the chief end of man is to glorify God and to enjoy him forever," worship might easily possess something like a central place in human culture. But in an age that has rather emphatically adopted the Baconian platform whereby "the kingdom of man founded on the sciences" is reckoned the really plausible end of man,[4] worship will become progressively irrelevant in proportion as the sufficiency of the program and its claims win general acceptance.

One recognizable fact about the recent past is that Bacon's program triumphed. Perhaps the distinguishing fact about the modern world is that the blueprint of human effort sketched in Bacon's *Novum Organum* — along with its method of implementation — has been generally accepted as defining the chief end of man. The "investigation of nature" and the method of "induction" are ways of implementation; and, as Bacon had hoped, they are the principal sources of the fabulous achievements of our present-day technologies.[5]

As Bacon foresaw and urged, technology affords all those "inventions and discoveries" through which man can exercise control over the given world and so exchange his humiliating subserviency for mastery.[6] The "true and lawful goal of the sciences," he declared, "is none other than this: that human life be endowed with new discoveries and powers."[7] Such knowledge is power, and, "by submitting the mind to things," Bacon hoped to "lay more firmly the foundations, and extend more widely the limits of the power and greatness of man."[8] He observed that "blind and immoderate zeal in religion" had long impeded the advance of natural philosophy.[9] But, if, by a proper division of labor, intelligence were directed to God's Work and faith devoted to his Word, no conflict need arise.[10] The range of reason was to be limited by "religion" and all ensuing knowledge was to be "referred to use and action."[11] If it was protested "sense doth discover natural things, but darken and shut up divine," then, in matters of divinity, Bacon is content to rely upon Bible, faith, and religion, thus liberating reason for its proper business.[12] Meanwhile the sciences would assure man's greatest ambition, namely, his "endeavor to establish and extend the power and dominion of the human race itself over the universe." [13] It was a prospect so beneficent in Bacon's eyes as to suggest fulfillment of the promise, "Man is God to man." [14]

Now were opened "horizons unlimited." Herewith humanity was promised emancipation from the fatalities of inscrutable circumstance, relief from the ravages of disease, and some deterrence of the relentless march of time. If, like Bacon, the modern devotee of technological progress does not expressly deny that "the chief end of man is to glorify God," for the most part he is so engrossed with the business that it hardly seems necessary. His denial is practical rather than theoretical. It just does not touch him that the Psalmist exclaims: "Lord, I have no good beyond Thee" (Ps. 16:2) or that another exults: "I will extol Thee, my God, O King; I will bless Thy name forever and ever" (Ps. 145:1). To St. Augustine's entreaty, "Let me know thee, O Lord, who knowest me: let me know thee as I am known of thee," the Baconian man is a stranger.[15] As a diligent and skillful trafficker in things visible, Augustine's confession passes him by: "Surely most unhappy is the man that knows all these things, and is ignorant of thee: but blessed is he that knows thee, though ignorant of these." [16]

Our age is the latest phase of an epoch which for about three hundred years has aggressively explored the adequacy of Bacon's program as the way of human fulfillment and, often unwittingly, as an alternative to worship. Its chief instrument, technology, is admirably suited to deal with the manageable, the predictable, and the usable. Its spectacular successes have, in turn, tended to entrench the conviction of both the ultimacy and the sufficiency of the spatio-temporal order; and, unexplored, the Transcendent has become progressively unthinkable. Given this context of existence, human effort is gauged in terms of efficient utilization of the environment; security is progressive control; fulfillment is maximum expansion and exploitation. The negations and limitations incident to physical being are successively overcome. If man's life continues to be imperiled by the relentlessness of time, man can at least extend his dominion by expansion, co-ordination, and utilization of space. These are the desiderata of the Baconian program for making-the-most-of this world. Utilization has been the shibboleth and exploitation the prevailing lust. The creatures are admired, but mainly for use.

Only in an ambiguous sense is it true of this epoch, as St. Paul testified of his, that men "exchanged the truth of God for a lie, and worshipped and served the creature rather than the Creator" (Rom. 1:25). The Baconian spirit may accord to the creature the acknowledgment hitherto reserved for the Creator. It may, as Augustine would have it, be wholly engrossed with the creatures; but the modern serves them mainly with a view to their utility. His worship is covertly self-service. When Western man in the seventeenth century came to extrude from the world all divine interposition and resolve providence into Laws of Nature thus to make his data wholly predictable, he was contriving the radical secularization of nature. With respect to nature he ceased to be husbandman and became *entrepreneur*. Nature became the arena of his exploitation for use. Unlike the ancient idolater, for whom nature was "full of gods" and worthy of reverence, the modern idolater attends nature only to serve himself. Thus even in his art he will not consent to being, that is, to the antecedent structure of nature. The object of art is dissolved after the imaginations of his own heart and replaced by the exuberance of his own thirst for self-expression. What he wants to see in his art is not nature but his reaction to nature. The progressive nullity of his art is a manifestation of his revolt against being.

Thus the spirit of our time is not consent to antecedent Being but arrogance toward beings, the creatures. The end of man is to be monarch of all he surveys. The world lies to hand to use and to possess. To this extent man accepts as he distorts the divinely conferred "dominion over the fish of the sea, over the birds of the heavens, over the cattle, over the earth, and over every creeping thing . . ." (Gen. 1:26). But, plainly, this is not the Biblical dominion. The latter is responsible dominion. It is known to be delegated, and the delegation of authority is acknowledged, first of all, in consent to Being.

The science of efficient utilization has been the undeclared messiah of Baconian secularism — the efficient management of spatial arrangements and resident powers of this world. It is the optimal utilization of space-time within the ineluctable limitation of the one-directional flow of time or biological duration. Whereas unsophisticated man, as Bacon complained,[17] capitulated too soon to the inscrutable and unmanageable restrictions of his existence and uncritically confounded the apparently unmanageable with the ultimately unmanageable, modern man begins by making a careful distinction. To the limits of his ingenuity, his aim is to manage the manageable and let the unmanageable take care of itself, that is, to endure it. This is secularism. It is the disposition to consent to Being only in its manageable appearances, and then to *assume*, rather than to *affirm*, that the appearances exhaust the sum of Being that man can or need know and with reference to which he can be gainfully employed. For these reasons worship is a word that, for the secularist, has become progressively devoid of meaning.

There is almost no way out of the circle of this mentality save through it. The destiny of modern man appears to be yet further exploration of his limited sovereignty until he is starkly and despairingly aware of its limitations. The conquest, the maximal utilization of space, with its reshaping and reorganization, will go on within the unconquerable delimitations of human biological time and private duration. But conquest takes time, more time than is given to any person, to any nation, to any people, to our planet. *Chronos* is our enemy, and, at the *finis*, there is only the ultimate enduring — the travail of the whole creation waiting vainly to be "delivered from the bondage of corruption." The alternative is worship, the consent of the human creature to the Creator. In this context, time may be seen as the indomitable manifestation of absolute Sovereignty with respect to which all human dominion is dependent and derivative. In this perspective, time is not the finality of endurance or the endurance of finality but the interval of God's self-revealing. For time is man's enemy, as the ancient myth has it, unless, as a signature of a more divine sovereignty, it prompts him to acknowledge the Eternal through its incontrovertible notice of the limits of all human duration.

The well-explored alternative to worship is, it may be said, the final endurance of meaninglessness. If the chief end of man is not to glorify God, then for Baconian man — and after all maximal utilization of

space — his proper *finis* is the embracement of noth-
ingness as his terminal gesture of resignation to the un-
comprehended and uncomprehending enigma of his
being anything at all. On the other hand, if St. Paul was
right, as Augustine believed, that "the invisible things
of him [God] since the creation of the world are
clearly seen, being perceived [i.e. perceivable] through
the things that are made," then a standpoint does exist
wherein the creation prompts to worship rather than
simply to exploitation. To recover this standpoint, to
subordinate utilization to consent to the being and in-
trinsic worth of the creatures is, perhaps, once again to
stand on the threshold of worship. For, in such a standpoint, there is implicit acknowledgment of the limits
of human sovereignty. This, in turn, may issue in man's
acceptance of responsibility for the exercise of such
sovereignty as he is entrusted with.

God is perhaps first known as the Limit set to man's
dominion and his limitless will to dominion. Worship
is nascent in the acceptance of limitation. It is maturing
in the acceptance of responsibility for the uses of freedom. It is perfected in the constant subordination of
self-affirmation to God-affirmation. Therefore, fulfilled worship is perfect obedience. From the standpoint of Christian faith, this is shown forth in the ministry of Jesus Christ; and, from that vantage point, all
other worship is participation in that ministry. For
the Christian, worship is acknowledgment of God

through the mediating vehicle of "the full, perfect, and sufficient Sacrifice."

III TOWARD FULFILLMENT OF WORSHIP

Worship, as has been summarily affirmed, is "acknowledgment of Transcendence." [18] The cogency of this claim is best seen by contrasting its import with the spirit and program of Baconian secularism in its full-orbed modern expressions. Transcendence, as Karl Heim long since pointed out, is precisely what contemporary man vainly strives to credit and ends by despairing of.[19] Worship, then, is easily the vocation of theonomous man, but he has become a declining species. In his place have arisen varieties of autonomous men who, deprived of transcendent reference and roots, are reduced to the initially exciting, but at length terrifying, destiny of promulgating the Law to themselves and determining the norms of truth, beauty, and goodness.

In the ensuing extremity of relativism and pansubjectivism, the various positivisms of the past century resorted to the expedient of redefining truth as the measurable and the useful, beauty as "significant form" that grasps one, goodness as the greatest good of the greatest number. Objectivity survived only in the sciences of measurement. In the sphere of human relations, morality was negotiable, as the conception of natural law, rooted in the *Logos* structure of Being, was replaced by the positive law of competitive nations. Where balancing of competitive claims proves infeasible, there has been but one appeal, as Plato long ago anticipated, namely, to that of superior power. Baconianism led to secularism and utilitarianism, the latter to positivism; and, all together led to the banishment of the Transcendent reference. So, as we find him today, modern man is struggling in his own power to establish a new positive law of nations, a "world rule of law," resting upon the consent of the governed, but on a world-wide basis. This is man's surviving and desperate hope, deprived as he is of the Transcendent and sentenced to his awful autonomy. The alternative to this may be the recovery of the Transcendent and, therewith, worship, as acknowledgment of the lawful structure of Being.

The Old Testament is replete with instances of man's temptation and overthrow, the fall by which he replaces a theonomous with an autonomous existence, and worships and serves the creature rather than the Creator. The word of the prophets is everywhere an indictment of idolatry and a call to return from the service of multifarious not-gods to responsible acknowledgment of the one God. Everywhere the prophets enforce the view that the first, the commanding, the finally decisive business of man is the acknowledgment of God. However man might traffic with the creatures and exercise his will over them, he profited from them and exercised his authority under the divine dominion. Thus, the first fruits of the earth and the firstlings of the flock were sacred unto the Lord, and man might not appropriate them without first acknowledging both their derivation and his divine authorization to possess and partake of their bounty. Thus sacrifice was overt acknowledgment of the prior ownership and sovereign goodness of God and also man's acceptance of his stewardship of the creatures.

At its heart, therefore, Old Testament worship was dyadic in nature or double-sided. It entailed, on the one hand, consent to God's sovereign being, majesty, and beneficence. It was praise and thanksgiving in reverence and adoration and in confidence, mingled with awe. But, on its other and empirically weaker side, worship was acceptance of responsibility for the uses of the divine benefits. Thus, a great part of the prophetic criticism was that worship was imperfect insofar as men did not adequately praise God by the way in which they administered their portion of the divine largess. True worship was abridged or nullified in those of whom Amos alleged that they "sold the righteous for silver, and the needy for a pair of shoes" (Amos 2:6), or of whom it was charged, they "trample upon the poor, and take exactions from him of wheat . . ." (Amos 5:11).

To the prophetic mind it was all too apparent that

sacrifices of "burnt offerings and meal offerings" were but token and calculated obedience, ostentatiously substituting for the whole of it. Accordingly, Amos and Isaiah concur in declaiming against the "multitude of sacrifices" and the pretentious noise of "solemn assemblies" (Isa. 1:11) — which, in making loud protestations to God, presume to distract his attention from the shoddiness of men's common lives. Against this subterfuge, that is mainly self-deception, there is sounded the divine imperative: "Let justice roll down as waters, and righteousness as a mighty stream" (Amos 5:24). Or Isaiah admonishes: "Wash you, make you clean, put away the evil of your *doings* from before mine eyes; cease to do evil; learn to do well; seek justice, relieve the oppressed, judge the fatherless, plead for the widow" (Isa. 1:16–17).

Contrary to an earlier mode of interpretation, this message of prophecy is not to be regarded as outright repudiation of sacrifice as such — sacrifice considered as appropriate acknowledgment of the divine favor. It is, rather, radical criticism of sacrifice in as much as it proffers itself as substitute for the whole of worship, namely, for that entire responsibility under God which acknowledges not only the Giver but the Giver's intention for the right uses of the gift. Sacrifices were abominations in so far as they were, wittingly or unwittingly, elaborate devices to disguise incomplete acceptance of the total responsibility that God enjoined.

So far forth, sacrifice was "phoney" worship, the counterfeit of entire devotion; and Amos might unleash his irony: "Come to Beth-el, and transgress; to Gilgal, and multiply transgression; and bring your sacrifices every morning. . . . for this pleaseth *you*, O ye children of Israel, saith the Lord!" (Amos 4:4, 5). It was plain to Amos that the dust raised by professional worship and intended for God's eyes is actually blinding only to those of the worshippers.

It is, perhaps, from this standpoint that we may see more narrowly into the substance of the *apocalypsis* which overwhelmed Isaiah in the Temple. Only the threefold seraphic *sanctus* could denote the unutterable Holiness which, unveiled to him, disclosed the uncleanness of all things human and shattered every presumption of the adequacy of man to find favor with God in his own strength. Supported by the whole array of the resplendent cultus round about him, neither the prophet nor his people could stand unrefined before the withering fire of the divine sanctity. Rudolf Otto once described this Presence of Holiness as the *mysterium tremendum* charged with indefectible moral rectitude. From Isaiah's own testimony, in the presence of the Holy Other, the profanity and uncleanness both of the prophet and of his people were revealed by sharpest contrast. Nothing now, not even the cultus of the Temple, could obscure the fundamental contrariety and alienation of man's being from the goodness of sanctity by which he was confronted. The confrontation was negation. Thus, in the presence of God, man's acknowledgment must first of all take the form of contrition and repentance. But the Holy One not only negates; He also reaffirms through cleansing, as fire that destroys also refines and purifies in refining. And, with cleansing, there is renewal; and, with renewal, there is acceptance of responsibility commensurate with the Holiness that bestows pardon. Thereupon comes the consciousness of election: "Whom shall I send, and who will go for us? Then I said, Here am I; send me" (Isa. 6:8).

We may be permitted to believe that through Isaiah's shattering and renewing experience in the Temple, Old Testament worship took a momentous step toward delocalization, moralization, and dematerialization. Far off down the same road, worship was to be "in spirit and in truth." Worship was no longer to be gifting of gifts, but entire responsibility based upon a prior acceptance of forgiveness and transformation of being. Worship was to become the giving up of oneself. Worship could no longer be a bargaining through which, by acknowledging primary dependency upon God, men could forestall additional and unwanted claims. Worship was now the entailment of the whole man, not the meted out apportionment of his goods in "the nicely calculated lore of more or less." [20] Worship meant entire obedience or conformity of life to the sanctity of goodness by which man is confronted. Worship was on the way to becoming in the words of the Edwardian liturgy, "the full, perfect, and sufficient sacrifice." It was on the way to becoming what we may call, awkwardly no doubt, *enpersonalized*. This obtains in the measure that man's acknowledgment of God commandeers his whole life and action. As consent to God's being, it is also consent to the kind of Being God is. But it is more: worship becomes enpersonalized when the injunction "ye shall be holy as I am holy" has become a personal aspiration in process of realization. In this emphasis, the "Priestly tradition" perpetuates the meaning of Isaiah's revelation.[21]

Enpersonalization of worship means what is plainly implied in Calvin's words, "true worship consists in obedience alone." [22] But "obedience alone" is fundamental conformity between the will to adore and the will to conform the life to the Adored. It is assimilation of the whole life to the likeness of Him who is magnified.

Thus, worship has always two aspects or, as it were, two directions. As, in the case of Isaiah, it exalts the Holiness of God and, then, cleansing following upon repentance, it brings "forth fruits worthy of repentance." [23] It is the inseverable connection between these two moments which constitutes authentic worship. This the prophets saw, and they resisted every divorcement of the two. With similar understanding, the classic words of the psalmist enforce the point: "For thou delightest not in sacrifice, else would I give it. Thou hast no pleasure in burnt offerings. The sacrifices of God are a broken spirit: A broken and a contrite heart, O God, thou wilt not despise" (Ps. 51:16–17). Worship is the penitential commitment of the whole life. Gone forever is the notion that worship is a certain measure of theonomy through which man reserves a measure of his autonomy. Wherever autonomy is reserved worship is imperfect and, in varying degree, idolatrous. The prophets perceived that the prevailing sacrificial cult, as a substitute for entire obedience, was a device for reserving man's autonomy to himself and, therefore, partook of essential idolatry.

The outcome is, then, that the prophetic invective against sacrifice and the attendant call to righteousness actually rested upon a deeper understanding of sacrifice itself. Sacrifice is the obedience of the whole life, the sacrifice of "a broken and a contrite heart," at once abased and exalted, by an overpowering awareness of the Divine Holiness. True worship becomes magnifying God's will by doing it or revering his Holiness in being conformed to his image. Its aspiration is expressed by the prayer of General Thanksgiving: ". . . that we may show forth thy praise, not only with our lips, but *in our lives,* by giving up ourselves to thy service, and walking before thee in holiness and righteousness all our days; . . ." It is the disparity between lip-service and life-service which is the recurring temptation of every established cultus, whereby it earns the displeasure of God and the eventual contempt of men.

Among the reformers, Calvin is notable for his insistence that true worship is obedience to both tables of the Law. While this may have issued in the legalistic excesses of later Puritanism, Calvin's instinct was reliable. Worship is first of all entire obedience or consent to the sovereign Being of God. It is fulfillment of the first commandment, summarized in the *Shema:* "Hear, O Israel, the Lord our God is one Lord: and thou shalt love the Lord thy God with all thy heart, and with all thy soul, and with all thy might" (Deut. 6:4). Since God is one, his proper acknowledgment entails a corresponding unification of the whole life around and upon its divine center. Worship, appropriate to the one God, can tolerate no competitors. But worship possesses a complementary aspect because the one God is a gracious God, which is to say that entire consent to God's sovereignty is also consent to his gracious intention toward the creatures and, among the creatures, other men. Entire obedience, therefore, embraces the second table of the Law and enjoins, as Isaiah perceived, conduct of life in righteousness. This is epitomized in the "second commandment" of our Lord: "Thou shalt love thy neighbor as thyself" (Matt. 22:39). The whole of worship is entire obedience to the two commandments — not complementary, merely, but inseparable.

This is, of course, the plainest import of the emphasis upon the "new commandment" in the Johannine writings. To worship the Father "in spirit and in truth" is almost certainly to unite love of God and love of man in such a fashion as that the one without the other is inconceivable. So to be understood is the startling declaration of the First Epistle: "If a man say, I love God, and hateth his brother, he is a liar" (1 John 4:20). The full exhibition of perfect obedience is reserved for the New Testament. It involves sacrifice, the sacrifice of all reservation of man's autonomy to theonomy.

The aspiring failure of worship under the old covenant is plain to Jeremiah, who looked forward to the fulfillment of true worship under a new covenant that God would yet establish: "But this is the covenant that I will make with the house of Israel after those days, saith Jehovah: *I will put my law in their inward parts, and in their heart will I write it;* and I will be their God, and they shall be my people" (Jer. 31:33). So the prophet looks to the day when the acknowledgment of God is not enjoined upon men but springs naturally from a resident impulse imparted by God's Spirit. He looks to a time when service of God issues from and invokes the whole man in personal response. Herein real community between God and man exists, in the Law written on the heart, in openness to and answerable existence under God. To say that such worship is enpersonalized is to say that worship has become community between man and God — love answering to love.

IV THE FULFILLMENT OF WORSHIP

Somewhat plainly, the indication of this paper is that there is no radical discontinuity between worship in the Old Testament and that in the New; there is only the incomprehensible "mystery of Godliness" which is the impenetrable mystery of the fulfillment of true worship in Jesus Christ. This, of course, is not to say that there are not all kinds of discontinuity between the prevailing cultic practices of post-exilic Judaism and the worship that gradually emerged in Christ's name, the worship of the early Church. Enormous differences there were that admit of meticulous delineation by those who make a business of these matters. Mooted may be the question of Jesus' attitude toward the Temple worship and sacrifice. Less questionable is the issue of his disposition toward the scribal refinements of the Law. But one thing is plain in the light of his own ministry: he came not to destroy the Law and the prophets but to fulfill (Matt. 5:17). If worship is properly understood as to its essence in the Old Testament, namely, as wholly responsible existence under God, as love to God and acceptance of God's will for the neighbor, or, if worship is understood as sacrifice of the self entire to the Divine purpose, then it is manifest that, as our Lord fulfilled in his own ministry the two commandments "on which the whole law hangeth and the prophets" (Matt. 22:40), he also fulfilled in his own person the meaning of worship or true service to God. But he did not reject sacrifice; he embodied it so that in him there is the final enpersonalization of worship. The truth in sacrifice he conserved and so fulfilled; its profusion of pretentious objectivities, overlaying and obscuring its essential validity, he rejected without comment. Our Lord perceived what the prophets had adumbrated, that cultus can be substitutional objectification of an act which, properly, can only be a personal commitment, that the sacrifices of God are a broken spirit, a humble and a contrite heart.

This sublimely lucid but basically simple comprehension of the meaning of man's service to God was to constitute the mastering motive of Jesus' existence. Worship is simply life that, in entire trustfulness, is given back into the hands of Him who gave it. But what is moderately simple to understand becomes thereafter, in the ministry and death of Jesus Christ, the miracle of its being enacted.

As the author of Hebrews so well understood, all surrogates of true sacrifice — the blood of goats and bulls, the altar, the veil, the Temple itself — are outward images of the fulfilled sacrifice of him who, once for all, offered up himself (Heb. 7:27). In Christ, sacrifice is enpersonalized. No longer a transaction *without*, in relation to which every man may remain safely a spectator, in Christ sacrifice is enacted all the way from acceptance of Sonship, entire serviceability, in his baptism, through the temptation of the whole wilderness way of his mortal days, to the final commitment of Gethsemane and the death of the Cross. And, with it all, there was a community with the Father and assimilation to his likeness that has left mankind through the ages utterly astonished and hung between incredulity and adoration. Far from being Platonist, the author of Hebrews understands with unexampled clarity that Christ gave sacrifice its personal embodiment and therefore its historical reality by contrast with which all outward sacrifices are but poor and partial images of the true. Henceforth the sacrifice of the altar is but a symbol of the sufficient sacrifice, the sacrifice of human autonomy without reservation.

Viewed in the perspective of Jesus' own proclamation of the Kingdom and his call to men to enter it by way of *metanoia* and acceptance of its rigorous demands (Luke 14:26–27, 33). Jesus' sacrifice may be interpreted as his own unfaltering decision, at every step of the way, to be wholly the Son to the Father. But the historical life of the elect One was existence in continuing temptation, while in every moment, from his baptism to Gethsemane, his victory over temptation was through steady acknowledgment of the Father's sovereign will. Thus, his ministry was service to God through victory in continuing temptation, so that, in the shadow of the Cross, he could say to his disciples, "ye are they that have continued with me in my temptations" (Luke 22:28). And, in the same moment, he had declared, "but I am in the midst of you as he that serveth" (Luke 22:27).

Refusal to accept "the transvaluation of values" explicit in this passage and that of Mark 10:42ff., as grounded in the most primitive gospel tradition, is to render the emergence as well as the peculiar offense of Christianity unintelligible. "Whosoever would be great among you shall be your minister (*diakonos*), and whosoever would be first . . . . shall be servant (*doulos*) of all," and "the Son of Man came not to be ministered unto but to minister. . . ." That these words embody the *scandalon* of the Gospel was plain equally to St. Paul and to Nietzsche. That their inherent logic is the Cross is also evident. That Jesus' baptism meant serviceability unto death is still visible in his words, "I have a baptism to be baptized with; and how am I straitened till it be accomplished" (Luke 12:50). Thus the meaning of baptism is ministry, and the issue of ministry is sacrifice, that is, if we are to understand our Lord's service in the context of the ancient Hebrew *leitourgia*, and we can hardly avoid it.

As heirs of the Enlightenment and its aftermath, we

moderns are virtually incapable of attaining to the realism of Jesus respecting the warfare between God and anti-god as constituting the basic antinomy of human existence. Therefore, we fail to credit Jesus with the lucid realization that, in the show-down with intrenched and acculturated demonic forces, the destiny of unarmed righteousness is death. In this world there is no place for Christ save as the Christ overcomes the world, and save as a Power greater than the world makes a place. Death can be victory only as it is *self*-sacrifice, offered unto God on behalf of those in bondage to fear of death. Likewise a place is made only through the perfect obedience, the apparent defeat, of the one man Jesus Christ. To the early Church these things signified the establishment of the "new covenant" and included realized community between God and man as the now accomplished desideratum of the ages. It was effected through the perfect *latreia* or ministry of Jesus called Christ.

The worship of the early Church was determined and shaped by the impact of this configuration of events upon those who, as witnesses, also received it in faith. If we are permitted to make a somewhat artificial differentiation, it was rather more the fulfilled mission of Jesus than his message which evoked faith. The remembered message more or less adequately, no doubt, illuminated "the mystery of Godliness" that he embodied; but in retrospect it was the total deed-event which evoked faith; and so entirely did his life embody the bearing of his own words that message and mission resolved into an abiding and redemptive unity. For the faith of the early Church, the unity was the ministry of Jesus, an unreserved stewardship of the whole of life. In it the true *latreia* of God was fulfilled, for the Law was fulfilled in its two modal aspects. Here was the ministry of the new covenant, not of the letter but of the Spirit.[24]

The faith that perceives this does so in the perspective of the history of redemption against the background of the imperfect *leitourgia* of the old covenant of which earlier prophecy served continual notice. The public rehearsal of the aberrations of traditional worship made Stephen the first Christian martyr. In his declaration, "Howbeit the Most High dwelleth not in *houses* made with hands," he joins himself not only to the ancient protest of prophecy but, we are bound to believe, gives earliest expression to the emerging Christian understanding that God resists domestication in any house save in the heart of living men.[25] Therefore, in the same letter to the Corinthians in which St. Paul speaks of "epistles" (i.e. testaments) written not in tables of stone "but in tables that are hearts of flesh" (3:3), he also speaks of the new people as "a temple of the living God; even as God said, I will dwell in them, and walk in them; and I will be their God, and they shall be my people." [26]

For Paul, the true *leitourgia* of God is a life of faith, a life indwelt by the Spirit of Christ that shows forth "the fruits of the Spirit" (Gal. 5:22). Accordingly, essential worship is suggested in Paul's entreaty to the Romans: "I beseech you therefore, brethren, by the mercies of God, to present your bodies *a living Sacrifice*, holy, acceptable to God, which *is* your reasonable service" (Rom. 12:1).

How shall we escape the implication that this service is the proper worship of God, since it is participation in the likeness of Christ's ministry of sacrifice? This day-by-day service of living sacrifice — manifesting itself in the righteousness of faith, hope, and love — is to be compared with 1 Peter 2:4-5. Here too Christ is "the *living* stone" to be contrasted with the stones of the earthly Temple. He is rejected of men but elect of God and, in his image, the people of God too are "living stones" who are "built up a spiritual house, to be a holy priesthood, to offer up spiritual sacrifices to God through Jesus Christ" (cf. Heb. 12:28). Herewith the worship of the early Church is seen to be radically enpersonalized. Worship is the service of the whole life.

The outcome seems to be that the worship of the early Church is what it is just exactly through Jesus Christ. It is an image of its original, and its original is none other than the ministry of perfect obedience. Christian worship is participation in the sacrifice of Christ, which supersedes all sacrifices and establishes a new covenantal relationship between God and men.[27] This is the bearing of the Epistle to the Hebrews: "For such a high priest became us, guileless, undefiled, separated from sinners, and made higher than the heavens; who needeth not daily, like those high priests, to offer up sacrifices, first for their own sins, and then for the sins of the people: for this he did once for all, *when he offered up himself*" (Heb. 7:26). St. Paul puts the matter succinctly: "For our passover also hath been sacrificed, even Christ: *wherefore* let us keep the feast, not with old leaven, neither with the leaven of malice and wickedness, but with the unleavened bread of sincerity and truth" (1 Cor. 5:7).

But Christian worship is not simply thanksgiving, although it is never less than that. Nowhere more than in the Johannine writings does it become clear that Christian worship is love answering to love. "We love, because he first loved us" (1 John 4:19). But, further, we cannot love God and fail to love what he loves, namely, the brother (1 John 4:7). Therefore there is the new commandment "that he that loveth God love his brother also" (1 John 4:21). In the new commandment are united the two on which hang the whole Law and the prophets.

But the worship of the early Church contains something more, namely, the *ways* in which the perfect obedience of Christ is appropriated by the believer. If forgiveness of sins and reconciliation to God through Christ are experienced in the early Church, then faith is not simply belief about; it is rather participation in the reconciling and redemptive event itself. This accounts for the centrality both of baptism and of the Lord's Supper in the Church's worship.

In baptism, the one who heeds the Word in repentance is participant in that baptism with reference to which our Lord said he was "straitened till it be accomplished." Thus, St. Paul identifies baptism with the dying of Christ; and in baptism we are united with him in the likeness of his death (Rom. 6:4, 5). While this signifies death to sin, it is at the same time acknowledgment of God in the life. It is intentional recapitulation of Christ's *latreia;* only it is "a living sacrifice."

With the Lord's Supper we also "proclaim the Lord's death till he come" (1 Cor. 11:26). Whatever more the Eucharist may have come to signify, it signified to the early Church the Lord's own invitation, indeed command, to participate with him in his "full, perfect, and sufficient sacrifice." Through such recurrent participation he unites believers to God by the mediation of his own self-offering, and by evoking in them, through his Spirit, the will to self-commitment like to his own. In the Eucharist men are enjoined again and again both to offer up the offering of Christ's perfect obedience and to be themselves wholly conformed to the likeness of his sacrifice.

The worship of the New Testament is celebration of the fullness of sacrifice. It is the unreserved acknowledgment of God accomplished in Jesus Christ and, through him, made possible as the vocation of every man. Worship is living sacrifice, a way of life open to the humble and the contrite heart — but a heart moved to contrition by "the glory of God in the face of Jesus Christ." Christian worship consists of "spiritual sacrifices, acceptable to God through Jesus Christ," that is, acceptable because of his sacrifice and, then, because these sacrifices are images united to his sacrifice. Or, finally, Christian worship is service of God through fellowship (*koinonia*) with, or participation in, Christ's suffering (Phil. 3:8ff.).

To sum up, in "the full, perfect, and sufficient sacrifice" of Jesus Christ, the whole meaning of the Law is fulfilled, in unfaltering love of God and in unhesitating love of man. This is the enpersonalization of worship; therefore the early Church saw it as God's own deed. God himself set forth this sacrifice to be an "expiation" for sin available to those who received it in faith (Rom. 3:25). The true worshipper is, first, Jesus Christ himself, and true worship is attained for those who, "crucified with Christ," walk in newness of life. This is life in which God's dominion is regnant. It is life in which autonomy is no longer reserved, and in which the stewardship of all of life is acknowledged.

NOTES

1. *Conatus* is here used as thrust toward fulfillment or completion of being. Employed by Spinoza, it signifies the endeavor of each thing to persevere in its being and as such is identical with the "essence" of the thing (*Ethics*, Bk. III, props. vi–viii). The distinctive *conatus* of man is constant "intellectual love of the mind toward God" (Bk. v, prop. xxxvi). Spinoza recognized, however, a disparity between reality and perfection in the case of man, but it was rather in his bondage to the "passions" than to self-will, as in the Christian Fathers. For discussion see the author's article "A Study of Freedom and Grace," *Journal of Religion*, xxv (1945), 209–12.

2. Plato's *Gorgias*, 482 a–c.

3. A phrase borrowed from Karl Heim in *Christian Faith and Natural Science* (SCM Press, 1953), pp. 20f.

4. Francis Bacon, *Novum Organum, Works*, ed. J. Spedding, (Boston, 1863), VIII, 99.

5. Cf. *Novum Organum*, p. 138.

6. Ibid. pp. 67, 206.

7. Ibid. p. 113.

8. Ibid. pp. 144, 145.

9. Ibid. p. 124.

10. *The Interpretation of Nature, Works*, VI, p. 29.

11. Ibid. p. 28.

12. Ibid. p. 29.

13. *Novum Organum*, p. 162.

14. Ibid.

15. *St. Augustine's Confessions*, x, 1.

16. Ibid. v, 4.

17. *Novum Organum*, p. 125.

18. Evelyn Underhill, *Worship* (Harper, 1937), p. 3; cf. Calvin, *Institutes of the Christian Religion*, I, iii, 1.

19. Cf. *God Transcendent* (Scribner's, 1936), pp. 35–40.

20. Wordsworth's line in the sonnet "On Trinity College Chapel."

21. Lev. 11:44; cf. 1 Pet. 1:15.

22. *Institutes*, II, viii, 5.

23. Luke 3:8; cf. Eph. 5:9.
24. Cf. II Cor. 3:3ff. and Heb. 8:6ff.
25. Cf. Heb. 9:11–15.
26. II Cor. 6:16b; cf. I Cor. 3:16–17.
27. In his famous sermon "The Circumcision of the Heart" (1733), John Wesley declared: "Other sacrifices from us he would not; but the living sacrifice of the heart he hath chosen. Let it be continually offered up to God through Christ." *Sermons*, II, 154.

J. COERT RYLAARSDAM

The Matrix of Worship
in the Old Testament

The matrix of worship in the Old Testament, the
key to its meaning and purpose, is most succinctly and
comprehensively summed up in Deuteronomy 6:4,
"The LORD our God is one LORD." This initial pro-
nouncement of the *Shema*ᶜ is the warrant for the imperatives that follow. In the Old Testament the unity
of God is not an abstract concept or principle but a
declaration of the LORD's transcendent freedom, syn-
onymous with the confession of God as Creator. The
effective meaning of all natural processes and of all
human actions, including those of worship, is not inherent to them but is resident in the will of God. The
processes of nature produce or effect what God ordains; and the forms of common life, both in society
and in worship, are the "ordinances of God." Whatever the cultural context or antecedent role of specific
phenomena or practices, the confessional import of
the *Shema*ᶜ is of overriding importance with respect

to their meaning in Israel. In the last analysis their significance and function is an inference from Israel's
account of the work of God. When in Israel's worship
this centrality and freedom of God were obscured, the
result was idolatry and magic; for us to overlook it in
our assessment of her worship is to attempt to understand the cultus of Israel without reference to the distinctive factor in Israel's faith.

I

In the concrete practice of Israel's faith proclamation
is the feature that especially illustrates the unity of
God as the key to Israel's worship. We have just noted
that in the *Shema⁰* the declarative is a basis for the imperative. This is also true in the Decalogue. Today,
thanks to the research of scholars such as Noth, the
notion prevails that the most solemn rite in ancient
Israel was a "covenant renewal ceremony." The thesis
is that the institution of the covenant was not simply
solemnized at a single initial rite, at Sinai. Rather, it
was celebrated annually, or, perhaps, every seven years,
at a central shrine to which pilgrimage was made. An
important feature of such a covenant renewal ceremony was the reading of the Law, by the observance
of which the Covenant would yield its promised blessings. It is possible to view the hortatory sermons of
Deuteronomy, with their threats and promises to make
urgent the call to obedience, as a literary reflection of

such a covenant ceremony. But while the blessings of the Covenant depend upon Israel's faithfulness, its establishment (and renewal) rests on the prior redeeming power and faithfulness of God. The celebration and proclamation of the Covenant that God ordains lie at the heart of the hypothetical "renewal ceremony." The "recital" of the great acts of God, in Israel's historic redemption and in the creation and rule of the world, points to the real substance of the Covenant; thus worship is the proclamation of the LORD in his power and goodness (Exod. 34:6f.).

Next to the opening of the *Shema*ᶜ, the most arresting example of this proclamatory dimension in Israel's worship is the preface to the Decalogue: "I am the LORD thy God that brought thee up out of the land of Egypt." Here the reference is to Israel's own history; and this is characteristic. The exhortations in Deuteronomy 1–11 also appeal to the great acts of God in behalf of his people. In Deuteronomy 26:1–11 we find a ceremonial prescription for the offering of the first fruits; the season for this offering began with the Feast of Weeks (Pentecost) and ended with Tabernacles. The individual worshipper presenting the grain to the priest announces the fulfillment of the promise, "I declare this day to the LORD your God that I have come into the land which the LORD swore to our fathers to give us." Then, when the priest has received and presented the offering, he gives a liturgical summary of the triumph of God in the history and redemption of Israel, beginning: "A wandering Aramean was my father . . ." (Deut. 26:5–10).

As in Exodus 20:2 (cf. Deut. 5:2ff.), the "confession" in Joshua 24:2ff. is also a proclamation summarizing Israel's history. This function of historical recital in worship enables us to see the liturgical role of the so-called historical Psalms (78, 105, 106, 136; Exod. 15). Indeed, the comprehensive shape of the Old Testament as a history is determined by this close association of proclamatory testimony and the life of the community; it is *Heilsgeschichte*. In faith Israel evaluates history as fate transformed by God's providential action. The "hymns" in the liturgical poetry of Israel, and also the "thanksgivings," at least insofar as these have a communal reference, must, I feel, also be associated with this primary dimension of proclamation in Israel's cultus. They sing the praise of the power of the LORD as creator and ruler of the universe (e.g. Pss. 74, 104) as well as his redeeming role in the destiny of his people (cf. Ps. 68). The so-called enthronement Psalms (47, 93, 95–100) are proclamations of this sort, combining these universal and particular roles. Thanksgiving, like proclamation, highlights the freedom and action of God.

It has often been held that in its manner of relating the imperative to the declarative, or in its account of law and grace, the Old Testament tends to relegate the

latter to the past and concentrate on the demand of
God upon Israel in the present. Deuteronomy and all
writings produced under its perspective are commonly
given this sort of theological interpretation. The acts
of God brought Israel into being — long ago. As such
they constitute an indispensable gift of "enabling
grace." But they are separated from the situation of
Israel in the present and from the demand that confronts her; they no longer determine her destiny. A
superficial reading of Deuteronomic history makes this
interpretation plausible. It can perhaps also be shown
that certain movements in Judaism tended in this direction. This view of the matter is nevertheless mislead-
ing; it overlooks both the theocentricity and the eschatological quality of all biblical historiography. It
must be noted that in biblical history present and past
are indistinguishable; it celebrates the power and action of God in the past to proclaim it as a present and
imminent reality. The cultus, with its hymns and
thanksgivings, celebrates and "re-presents" both the
redemption and the judgment of the action of God.
The prose histories and the Deuteronomic sermons
recount the story of Israel's part up to the present moment, to focus upon the immanence of the divine advent which is the realization of the destiny of the
people of God. To be sure, the element of futurity
bulks large in this cultus, and the action of God, at
least in redemption, is contingent upon Israel's ex-

pectant faithfulness. But what it celebrates and proclaims is the certainty and adequacy of this action.

The great festivals — Passover, Weeks, and Booths
— like the national histories, also wipe out the distance
between past and present to proclaim the centrality
and freedom of God.

The priestly traditions in the Old Testament and
the Mishnah feature the Passover as a sacrifice and in
this way deeply influence the New Testament. The
blood of the lambs, ceremonially slain in the great court
of the temple, was tossed against the side of the great
altar of sacrifice (Pesah 5:5–10), and was the means
of declaring and releasing the redeeming action of God
for his whole people. Originally an apotropaic device
(Exod. 12:21–23) and later, perhaps, an individual
sacrifice to substitute for the first-born Israelite, it had
become the sign of God's imminent redemption. The
communal meal was, similarly, the anticipation of the
messianic banquet. The question about the meaning
of the feast (Exod. 12:26) introduces the historical
haggadah with its recital of the deeds of God. And the
meal concludes with a prayer for deliverance from the
Romans or for a return to the holy city. It may be
pointed out in this connection that Passover, like the
other great feasts, was a pilgrim festival and that in
the prophetic visions of the End, the final and victorious
pilgrimage, in which the remnants of the nations also
join, is a central feature (cf. Matt. 8:11).

The great bulk of references to the Passover treat it as a human action; i.e. Israel "keeps" the Passover, sacrifices it, etc. But in four instances (Exod. 12:11, 27; Lev. 23:5; Num. 28:16), probably all reflecting the Priestly traditions, this is not the case. In these we have the statement פסח הוא ליהוה (It is the LORD's passover). The title seems to refer immediately to the action of God in passing-over to smite the first-born of Egypt (Exod. 12:12). It may be noted that in this same context the institution of the feast takes place in anticipation of the deliverance (Exod. 12:6-7, 12-13).

The feast of Booths, probably the original pilgrimage festival, had its antecedents in a Canaanite vintage festival with pronounced bacchanalian features. In Israel the rite of the water procession from the Pool of Siloam and the circumambulation and libation of the altar continued to exhibit the forms of a rain-making ceremony with aspects of sympathetic magic that fit a setting in nature mysticism. Nevertheless, the theocentricity of Israel's faith transformed the meaning of every part of it. While marching around the altar the procession sang the Hallel (Ps. 113-118). At the opening of Psalm 118, at the words, "O give thanks unto the Lord," the worshippers waved their *Lulabs*, and again, with a great shout, at verse 25: "Save us, we beseech thee, O Lord," so that the whole rite came to be known from this shout as *Hoshianah Rabbah*. It is a cry for the action of God, not simply for an

annual cycle of rainfall, but for an eschatological fulfillment. Yet the rain ceremony with its initially limited
preoccupations and overtones of sympathetic magic
serves as the vehicle for this declaration of faith. The
magic is eliminated not by a change in form, but by
the antecedent confession that its effectiveness depends
on its divine institution.

Thus in their major facets these feasts are a dramatic
proclamation of an eschatological event effected by
the Action of God. But as a means of proclaiming the
Word (Action) of God they are simultaneously rites
that help to effect it; they help to accomplish what
they celebrate. Phenomenologically speaking, virtually
all forms and actions of the observances have a pre-
Israelite history as cultic rites. A plausible account of
their effectiveness can be given in terms of the context
of nature mysticism in which they originally functioned: but this overlooks the very important fact that
in the Old Testament the rites are always treated as
divine ordinances. They are the memorials and signs
the LORD has commanded Israel to observe and this
is the key to their meaning. In Israel, God is present
in the liturgical action of the cultus, in the material
forms it employs, and in the community of the covenant in its material and institutional existence, as well
as in the oracles of the prophet.

This "materialism" of Israel's cultus is a feature of
great importance to which we must give further at-

tention below. At this point we simply note that the effectiveness of all rites depends upon their status as ordinances willed by God. There is nothing inherently significant about the matter employed. This is most graphically illustrated in the treatment of the blood that is sprinkled on the Day of Atonement. In the liturgical action, the blood of the bull for the cleansing of the priest and that of the goat for the cleansing of the people are treated with the deepest reverence. As the tractate *Yoma* makes plain, there is the greatest circumspection about using it in the prescribed manner, to cleanse the officiants, the community, and the altar from the pollution of sin. Yet, in most startling contrast, the *Yoma* relates how the surplus was poured down a disposal channel that drained into the Kidron and that there the gardeners collected it for fertilizer. Clearly the cleansing virtue of the blood did not rest on the notion derived from nature mysticism that "the blood is the life" (though its presence in the cultus must be associated with that) but on the will of God who chose to use it. Even in the Epistle to the Hebrews the statements that the blood of Christ is superior to that of animals and that without the shedding of blood there is no remission of sins (Heb. 9) must, we feel, be read as a confession of faith about the will of God rather than as the outcome of an analysis of moral virtues. Looked at from an Old Testament point of view, the Epistle to the Hebrews (and many analogous parts of the New Testament) makes sense as a testimony to the Christian recovery of Israel's theocentricity; as a critique of the cultic institution of Israel, *per se*, its value is more dubious.

This radical theocentricity of Israel's cultus, which affords the basis for its proclamatory character, sets limits not only to the significance of the material forms employed, but also to that of self-conscious personal religious experience. We have just noted that there was no virtue in the blood of the sacrifices of the Day of Atonement, apart from liturgical actions in which it functioned. It must also be noted that a repentant spirit, however important and however genuine, was no substitute for the actual ceremony of Atonement. According to the Mishnah (Yoma 8:8f.) repentance was essential if one were to participate in the fruits of the Day of Atonement; on the other hand, not the repentance but the holy day and its ordinances effect atonement. True repentance by man could suspend punishment until the Day of Atonement. But only the action of God through and by the cultus and the priesthood he had instituted could wipe out man's sin. Israel's own interpretation of the Day guarded against what we would call "subjectivism." And they did so by exalting the action of God in and by the ordinance he had provided.

I I

The key to the understanding of Israel's worship is the kingship of Yahweh; and the primary corollary of this is the servanthood of Israel. Israel belongs to God, as servant and as son. Israel is a single entity, a whole that is antecedent to every Israelite. In the dramatic account of Yahweh's conflict with the Pharaoh, which is the Old Testament equivalent of the cosmic drama of the so-called Babylonian Creation myth in which Marduk overcomes the dragon, the ownership of Israel passes from the Egyptians to the LORD because he is triumphant. Israel is the booty Yahweh acquires as the prize of his victory. This is the way it appears from the outside, especially to Egypt. But for Israel this "conquest" is the liberation and redemption she has cried out for. Even while still in bondage to Pharaoh she grasps at the opportunity of entering the service of Yahweh; under Moses' tutelage, she chooses Yahweh as emancipator, co-operates in making good the divine triumph, and accepts the conditions of remaining in the possession and protection of God. Such is the election and the covenant.

Israel's status as the servant is cultically acknowledged in the rite of the first-born. Like the Passover, the institution of the consecration of the first-born is set in the context of the exodus (Exod. 13:1f., 11–16). It is a sign of the power of God (Exod. 13:14f.). There is considerable evidence for the view that the rite was originally an integral part of the Passover observance. Phenomenologically, of course, the rite had its roots in nature mysticism. It constituted a recognition of the mysterious vital forces resident in mutual processes that make possible and set limits to human existence, and commonly exhibited propitiatory intentions. But in Israel it is a way of saying that Israel belongs to God by virtue of God's power and that she freely acknowledges and rejoices in this relationship. Egypt — and all nations — also belong to God, as the slaying of the first-born demonstrated; but, unlike Israel, she resists God's rule. The first-born of animals as well as of man were consecrated to God; the first-born stands for the whole. God possesses all things: "For every beast of the forest is mine, the cattle on a thousand hills" (Ps. 50:10); it is the glory of Israel to be able to confess this.

The rite of the first-born not only proclaims God's possession of Israel; it also declares Israel's sonship. The basis of every sacrifice is the gift of God himself; and Israel exists by the grace of God. This is especially illustrated in the patriarchal stories in the manner in which the promise to Abraham is fulfilled. It is indeed seed of Abraham that inherits Canaan. But the story of the birth of Isaac (of which there is an echo also in the barrenness of Rebekkah) makes the point that even in its natural life, as well as in its escape from slavery and its conquest of Canaan, Israel exists by the grace of God and lives out of his power. The natural and historical forces of life are the means of the divine action; but, in contrast to the nature mysticism of Canaan, they are only means. The health of Israel is nowhere better illustrated than in its capacity to assimilate the cultic forms of Canaan and redefine their role in terms of her own faith.

This capacity for assimilation is even more graphically illustrated in the agriculturally related aspects of the cultus. The offering of "first fruits," i.e. of the grain harvest, complemented the sacrifice of the firstborn. Its distinctive role was to confess that not only Israel but also its land was the possession of God; and that the fertility of the soil, no less than that of man or beast, was a gift. As the Passover was probably originally the occasion for the offering of the firstborn, so Weeks or Pentecost was the feast of the grain harvest that featured the offering of the first fruits. It may be noted in passing that Weeks remained an agricultural feast during the entire Old Testament period, and that it was still such when the New Testament was written. The "historicizing" of the feast, as a commemoration of the giving of the Law did not occur until the second century of the Christian era, a fact which undercuts all traditional exegetical attempts to treat the Christian Pentecost as a dramatic Law-Spirit antithesis. It is rather the celebration of a fulfillment anticipated in every annual celebration of Israel's feast

of pilgrimage; and even though there is no reference
to the land and its fruits in the story in Acts, its very
association with the feast of Weeks suggests that the
Christian Pentecost is, at least by implication, also a
celebration of the redemption of nature wrought by
the risen Christ in the gift of the Holy Spirit.

As a feast, Weeks lasted only a single day (two
days in the Diaspora); but this day concluded a holy
season of fifty days that began with the ceremony
of the Barley Sheaf on the day after the "sabbath" of
Passover. These fifty days were a season of special
sanctity. With the waving of the barley sheaf it became possible for the people to harvest and eat of the
new crop; but not until Pentecost was it possible to
use the new grain in sacrifice. The ceremony of the
Sheaf was an integral part of Unleavened Bread; this
sheaf was the ἀπαρχή of both the holy land and of
all mankind (Philo, *De Septen.* 2:20; cf. 1 Cor. 15:20,
23) and is completed in the offerings of first fruits
seven weeks later. During this entire period the priests
seem to have abstained from eating leaven. It is evident how the taboos of an ancient nature mysticism
shine through at many points. Nevertheless, the complex and "pagan" forms of the rite were fully assimi-
lated and served to dramatize Israel's confession that
God was the Creator of heaven and earth who had a
covenant with his land as well as with his people, and
was the source of the fertility and power of both, using

both in the realization of his plan. "The earth is the
LORD's"; and he uses it.

III

The faith of Israel is an historical faith. We have noted
that in the "covenant ceremony" the recital of Israel's
own history as a record of the acts of God occupied
the central place. Martin Noth has detected four primary historical themes — patriarchs, exodus, wandering, conquest — as the framework for Israel's cultus.
The Old Testament's real counterpart to the Babylonian *Enuma Elish* is not the creation stories in Genesis
but the titanic struggle of Yahweh with the Pharaoh
of Egypt for the possession of his people. That struggle
is the occasion of his revelation and the establishment
of his universal authority. In the creation accounts of
Genesis there is no hint of a struggle; the authority
of the LORD is assumed. Israel's confession of God as
the ruler of nature is an inference from her confession
of his rule in history. It is only much later, in Jewish
apocalypticism, in the context of the dualistic influences
emanating from Iranian and other outside quarters,
that the rule of God over nature becomes problemati-
cal and is reaffirmed in dramatized accounts of a cosmic
struggle and triumph.

However, though the focal point of revelation was
historical and particular, our examination of Israel's
cultus thus far has already yielded abundant evidence

that there is no neglect of nature or universality. The faith and its cultus were indeed occasioned by the exodus; but its confession in the Pentateuch begins with Genesis. Yahweh discloses himself as Redeemer of Israel; but he is worshipped as Creator. He is the One who "visits" his people and who is nevertheless enthroned "above the flood." A perusal of the Psalter soon shows how these two factors of Israel's confession inform and support one another in the literature of worship. In effect, the line of demarcation between nature and history disappears, not simply because history is also involved in nature. To be sure, that "modern" notion has its equivalent in Israel (cf. Ps. 90). But the key to this co-ordination of nature and history in the Old Testament is the universality and authority of the rule of God. All peoples praise Him; and the little hills clap their hands. Israel greatly enriched the content of her own faith by assimilating and redefining the forms of Canaan's nature mysticism.

Interpreters of Israel's cultic history, notably under the influence of Wellhausen, have been greatly concerned to record the "historicizing" of the worship. Wellhausen developed the principle of "denaturierung" according to which the great pilgrim feasts, particularly, were very gradually transformed from nature feasts to memorials of Israel's history. Passover-Unleavened Bread and Booths were chiefly the subjects of this inquiry. (We have already seen that in the

case of Weeks the change did not occur until after
the beginning of Christianity.) In general the conclusions tended to the view that in the case of these two
the change did not really occur until the Reformation
of Josiah in the seventh century. Coupled with this
went the assumption that this "historification" of the
feasts was the definite index to their true assimilation
in the worship of Yahweh. Thus, it was intimated,
Israel's earlier worship of God as "the Lord of history,"
on the basis of the exodus, was never really more than
a tribal cultus. In the national consolidation this was
sidetracked almost completely in favor of the nature
mysticism of Canaan. The development of "monothe-
ism," according to this scheme, was the fruit of the
prophetic preaching which was institutionally imple-
mented by the Deuteronomic reformers. Under their
auspices Passover-Unleavened Bread and Booths finally
were transformed from Baalistic nature feasts into Yah-
wistic feasts celebrating Israel's history as the people
of God. Quite apart from its chronological conclusions, the Wellhausen thesis warps the meaning of
Israel's faith and worship by setting "history" over
against nature.

Today, as a part of the general reaction to the Wellhausen scheme, Hans J. Kraus is the leader of a movement that attempts to demonstrate that the feasts of
Passover-Unleavened Bread and Booths were treated
as commemorations of Israel's history from its earliest

days in the land of promise. The movement presupposes the amphictyonic notions of Alt and Noth, according to which, from the first, Israel as a worshipping community constituted a single entity that overcame all antecedent natural tribal divisions and outlined the political division of David's dominion into two separate kingdoms. There is much to be said for the views put forward, even though the concrete Old Testament evidence offered for the early historification of the Canaanite agricultural festivals is quite ambiguous. Whatever may be the final answer about the validity of the particular reconstructions made by Kraus, the current movement deserves great credit for reestablishing an empirical line of living tradition in Israel leading from the era of Moses to the time of Josiah's Reformation. The exodus faith belonged to the era of the exodus and did not begin with the eighth century prophets; nor was its dynamic significance ever obliterated in the days of the settlement and the early monarchy.

But what both the school of Wellhausen and the current movement tend to overlook is the fact that the so-called process of historicizing of the agricultural feasts did not constitute a displacement of their significance as observances of natural processes. In Israel the feasts that celebrated Israel's escape from slavery and her inheritance of Canaan were also feasts of natural fertility: seed-time and harvest, rainfall, oil, grain, and wine — these too were acts of God; and without them Israel's political and social existence loses its meaning. The order of Creation and the order of Redemption are held together: "God is One." In assimilating the nature mysticism of Canaan, Israel used it as a bridge to develop the confession of God as Creator. And the characteristic "materialism" of the Old Testament, according to which the presence and action of God are mediated by the cycles and processes of nature, owes not a little to the persistence of the forms and preoccupations of the cultus of Canaan in the worship of Israel. The central authority of God in both nature and history rather than the comparative role of the historical and the natural is the real cue to the uniqueness of Israel's worship. It may not be improper to point out that Christianity has perhaps never done full justice to its Old Testament heritage with respect to the role of nature, Protestant worship least of all. The "foxhole" prayers for rain by twentieth-century Christians, for whom nature is no longer alive with the power and action of the living God, are ridiculous; and they are both less authentic and less worthy than the procession from the Pool of Siloam in which the devotees waved their bundle of green twigs to which they had attached the ethrog as a symbol of fertility. Humanly speaking, the confession of the Incarnation could only have occurred on Old Testament soil. It offends the Jew not because it involves God in matter, but because it seems to compromise his unity. For many a Protestant Christian it is robbed of its meaning because he has lost the comprehensive significance of the Old Testament doctrine of Creation.

IV

We have described Israel's worship as eschatological. The term has certain connotations that make its use in the context of Old Testament interpretation questionable. In her cultus Israel celebrates the triumph of God as an actual fact, both in her own history and in creation. It also prays for and celebrates an anticipated triumph when all resistance to the will of God will have ceased, when the lion shall lie down with the lamb, and when nation shall no longer lift up sword against nation — when the knowledge of God shall cover the earth as the waters cover the bottom of the sea. Because of the centrality and unity of God, hope is expressed in terms of an absolute, a finality. In this sense we can speak of an eschatological dimension.

But this finality is conditioned throughout by the relativities of space and time. The realization of the End is envisaged as a goal *in* history; it is not a "new Jerusalem coming down out of heaven," but the vindication of a renewed Jerusalem on earth. Time and space belong to the end; so does the material and physical continuity of Israel as the people of God, a factor which enhances the materialism already alluded to. These belong to the End not in the sense that their *meaning* is subsumed in it, but in the sense that they belong to its *form*. One way of summing up the difference between the Old Testament and the New Testatment is to note that in the Old Testament the Elect One never dies. He may be reduced to a remnant, battered, despised, and rejected; but he is never annihilated as an historical entity. And the maintenance of his identity in time and space is the pledge of the realization of the hope; hence prayer, worship, and dedication all focus upon it. In Christianity, on the other hand, the Elect One dies; and faith proclaims his resurrection by the power of God as the realized goal of the Work of God by means of which man is released from what Eliade calls "the tyranny of history." Time and space, or the story of man in their context, can no longer affect the realization of man's hope. A Christian may say that his position in this respect does greater justice to the Old Testament affirmation of the unity of God than the Jewish view does; a Jew will reply that it does so both irrationally and irresponsibly. But here we must note that the difference deeply affects the cultus. It is this difference that is *really* involved when Christians, all too glibly, refer to Judaism as legalistic. We began by citing the confessional declaration of the *Shema*; it also has an imperative side, as do all the other "confessions." And these two are inseparable. The responsibility of the community of the covenant is warranted by the proclamatory announcement of Salvation; but the inexhaustible action of the living God makes use of and, from the human point of view at least, is bound up with and depends on the obedience of the people of God in history. Not only has history served the Kingdom of God; it does so now, and always will.

For Judaism the maintenance of the historical community of Israel is dictated by an insistence on the continuity *in* history between the event of revelation and the realization of its meaning. In the faith and worship of Israel hope is the greater word, not love. Hope is a duty and a dogma; the warfare of faith is the battle of hope. The Hebrew word for hoping (קוה) is also the word for waiting. Waiting — hope — is the central term in Jewish piety:

Wait for the Lord: be strong and let your heart take courage;
    yea, wait for the Lord (Ps. 27:14).

Rest in the Lord and wait patiently for him (Ps. 37:7).

My soul waits patiently for the Lord!
    More than watchmen for the morning (Ps. 130:6).

For Israel life is summed up in that single word, wait! It contains all the joy and exhilaration of faith; all the zest and purpose of living. It is a glorious thing to wait, for see what you are waiting for — the coming of the Kingdom of God. The struggles and tears of life have their compensation: the lash of the Assyrian and the sneer of the Greek; the gate of the ghetto and the gentlemen's agreement; L'Affaire Dreyfus and the Diary of Anne Frank — they all dissolve to nothing in the face of the prize to be won. "Wait for the Lord" — this is the watchword that makes endurance possible; but it does more, it provides an endless incentive to work, to exercise dominion of the world God has created.

But in Israel's piety there is a cry that beclouds this joy of waiting. This is a cry as old as Jeremiah; not the cry of the tortured and the slain, but the cry of delay and longing: "How long?"

My soul is sorely troubled . . . How long? (Ps. 6:3)
How long shall my enemy be exalted over me? (Ps. 13:2)
How long, O Lord, wilt thou be angry? (Ps. 79:5)
How long shall the wicked triumph? (Ps. 94:3)

Waiting can become an agony when it is stretched out in time. It is like chasing the rainbow's end, an endless pilgrimage documented in this century by Franz Werfel's "The Eternal Road." The cycles begin to repeat themselves, and the crises become recurrent. Sometimes the end seems very near and then, all of a sudden, it recedes again. But the lamp of faith is never quenched; each crisis is surmounted; and whether it be in Egypt, in Babylon, or in Warsaw, it is a sign that God is King and that hope is well founded.

If it had not been the Lord who was on our side;

Let Israel now say, If it had not been the Lord who was on
  our side, . . .

Then they would have swallowed us up alive. (Ps. 124:1f.)

So the pilgrimage goes on; the line that ties the present to the future is never broken. Faith is fixed on
the "Rock of Israel" and hope never dies; but in the
tyranny of history, it is mixed with agony. The face
of Jewish piety is quite unlike that of the Christian
saint. It is a face that bears the agony of the ages. It
is marked with the scars of the folly of all mankind,
including its own. It is not a face that has "let go,"
but that has endured. Look at Jewish art forms: the
lines on the face of an aged rabbi at prayer, or the
characteristic chords of the liturgy. The same bur-
den Christ bore in his death to bring an end to history
Israel has always borne and will always bear in history. The agony of Job, which is the tyranny of
history, still continues. Job was finally convicted of
presumption: repenting before God, he threw away
all blueprints and all timetables. But he did not cease
to hope — and work. And in so doing he set the course
for Israel's piety and life in a direction that has not
altered since.

In the Christian cultus the definition of a sacrament
is profoundly conditioned by the role of nature, on
the one hand, and by the eschatological character of
Christian faith on the other. The former is an Old

Testament legacy. Whenever Christians cease to define the meaning of nature as instrumental to the purpose and action of God, sacramental life atrophies; and when this action of God, in revelation and redemption, comes to be equated with a conscious, individual, "personal experience," sacraments are perforce dispensed with. Today there is ample evidence for this in American Protestantism. Neither a religion of the *spirit* nor a religion of the *Spirit* has need of a sacrament!

All of this, however, is reversed in the Old Testament. I doubt that it is possible or helpful to speak about sacraments, properly so called, in Israel's cultus. In fact, with the exception of the rites of the Day of Atonement, which were later, there seems to be very little excuse even to speak of sacramental action. Circumcision is not a sacrament analogous to Baptism; nor is Passover-Unleavened Bread or First Fruits a parallel to the Eucharist in this respect. And the difference inheres in the fact that in Israel the material forms and actions employed were themselves, as such, a part of the reality celebrated rather than the "signs" or vehicles of something else. The "End" for which Israel endured, its "eschatological hope," was in terms of a fulfillment of the plan of God *in* history and did not transcend the forms of time, space, or matter. Each Israelite born and circumcised was not just a "sign" of the fulfillment; he was a part of it, as such, in his

physical and earthly existence. Each new crop, ceremonially eaten, first without leaven and then with it,
was as such an ἀρραβών of the final hope; the "trans-
position" of meaning which is an aspect of a sacrament is uncalled for. Indeed, it is a mark of the difference between the Old Testament and the New
Testament, that Israel's faith and worship flatly reject
this. Such New Testament assertions as those about
being "in Christ" instead of "in the flesh" relate to
the same distinction.

V

We have tried to show that for Israel worship was
theocentric. It rested on the action of God. Indeed,
it was a proclamation of this action; and it came as a
response to it. Moreover, the God who evoked Israel's
worship was One. He was Creator. The structured
processes of nature — impersonal and personal, physical and psychic, material and cultural, participated in
his action and served as the instruments for it. This
participation and function, rather than anything inherent to them, *per se*, gave them their meaning. God
was also Redeemer, the Lord of history who brought
good out of evil. It was a part of his One-ness that
his action as Creator and as Redeemer was one action.
The Word belonged to God; and Israel whom he
had redeemed and called to participate and serve in
its redemption also belonged to him. Worship was

the celebration of this divine action, a participation
in it, a thanksgiving for it, and an acknowledgment
of obligation in relation to it. It was, above all, a proclamation of the adequacy of God's action; that is, it
was eschatological. The fullness of God's action was
an ever-valid Promise. Because God was One, his self-
revelation would not cease and his Redemption would
be realized.

How may this account of the worship of ancient
Israel guide American Protestants in their recovery
of an understanding of the meaning of Christian
worship? What important dimensions of the faith of
Christians, indicated by this rich legacy, fail to be
clearly proclaimed and celebrated in their worship?
What assumptions about Christian worship and what
aspects of its practice make difficult a fuller proclamation of the faith in it? In pondering these questions
it becomes clear that simply compiling a catalogue of
rites and ceremonies used, or of forms discarded, re-
tained, or rediscovered and reinstated, will not give
us adequate answers to our questions. The actual assumptions of the worshippers, expressed or unspoken,
about the range and nature of the work or Word of
God to be proclaimed and celebrated in worship are
much more decisive than the forms and rites used, or
the content of official confessions in determining
what will actually be "remembered" and communi-
cated. Criticism or change in the latter must rest on

an understanding and evaluation of the former.

In both its witness and worship Protestant Christianity in America is conditioned and formed by Pietism much more decisively than is the case in Europe.
As an examination of its popular hymnody shows, it
is preoccupied with the individual rather than with
the community as a whole, and with the response of
man to the action of God rather than with the proclamation of that action itself. The holiness and love of
God make way for the sanctification of the saved in
the spontaneous awareness of the worshippers; and
the sense of personal responsibility obscures the message of prevenient grace borne by Word and Sacrament. Worship is "experience-centered" and subjective, not only among the institutional heirs of Pietism
but also among the heirs of its opponents.

This turning away from the God-centeredness of
biblical worship, as exemplified by the *Shema*ᶜ, is
wholly inadvertent and "pious." It is not at all intended
as an act of rebellion or as a declaration of freedom
from God, but as a response to his love and goodness.
Yet it is nurtured by a seriously unbiblical or imper-
fectly biblical view of the work of God. For Pietism
the action of God tends to be equated with an individual person's conscious apprehension of it. Revelation is not an objective event involving the structures
and processes of time, space, and matter so much as a
personal and individual experience. Imperceptibly, the

theme of God the Creator is drained of its biblical meaning, and the Covenant, as applied to the people of God, is a result of personal redemption rather than the form for it. The presence of God in the world of nature and history is reduced to a reflection or projection of a Christian's experience of God. Thus the majesty of God the Creator and the mystery of God as Judge and Redeemer who makes even the wrath of men praise him are lost in human intimations of the true, the good, and the beautiful.

The practical consequence of the loss of the centrality and unity of God in the assumptions that condition our worship is what is popularly called secularism. The Psalmist's confession that, "The earth is the LORD's . . . The world and they who dwell therein"; i.e. that God is always and everywhere and in everything preveniently and dynamically present, no longer grips the imagination. The earth is just nature and the world is just people. God is, indeed, the Holy One; but all of his creation is not invested with this holiness. The awe of it is localized in the heart of the converted and through him the world and life must be sanctified. Arenas of human action, such as industry, politics, and marriage, are no longer objectively holy in the sense that they represent powers and means by which God also acts. They are only subjectively holy for the faithful who seek in and by them to bear a personal Christian witness.

Because it proclaims God as Creator of the universe and LORD of history Israel's worship never loses touch with the concrete material and social aspects of human existence. It proclaims a this-worldly faith, a faith that can even be called "materialistic" in the sense that revelation takes place in, through, and by means of the processes of time, space, and matter. Spirit is not separated from matter, nor eternity from time. Nature on all its levels — animate and inanimate, conscious and unconscious, sensitive and coarse — is serviceable to God who, in this tradition, finally becomes incarnate to live in time. But this temporal and material concreteness is lost when the celebration of personal Christian "experience" becomes focal in worship. Spirit is divorced from matter and the work of God becomes ethereal and evanescent, having little to do with harsh everyday realities. The sacraments become dedicatory rites and worship is transformed into an occasion for personal refinement and mutual exhortation.

Western civilization is often described as sensate and "materialistic" by its Oriental critics. Sometimes Christians join these critics too easily. In the account of creation in Genesis man is given "dominion . . . over all the earth" in its material fullness. It is his to exploit and use, as a participant with God in the attainment of his destiny. The people who wrote the Bible were not scientists or technologists. But in their witness to God as Creator they provided both with a practical motive and a theological basis. Given the doctrine of Creation there is a sense in which this so-called sensate and material side of our culture is both imperative and inescapable. The recovery of the full biblical dimension of the meaning of God as Creator of heaven and earth is the one sure shield against that reductionist materialism which makes man's technological mastery of his material work self-explanatory. The Christian answer to Communism lies not primarily in the popular humanist notion about the freedom and dignity of man but in the affirmation of God as the Creator who participates in and uses the order of nature as the scene and means of his action.

There was a time, still remembered by some of us, when poets and thinkers were optimistic about what man could do for himself in relation to his environment. "Glory to man in the highest," sang Swinburne, "for man is the master of things." And Lord Tennyson dreamed of "a parliament of man" by which man's reason and judgment would vindicate his prowess and make him master of history as well. Other poets, less hopeful, have displaced these: Robinson Jeffers, Robert Penn Warren, and many more. Western man today is soberly realistic about his powerlessness. He knows that the course of his life is set and predetermined by forces he can hardly influence at all. The implications of the work of men such as Marx, Freud, and Einstein have deeply influenced the popular imagination. Sometimes one is jolted to discover that about the only place in which the old-fashioned man-centered optimism still survives is in the Protestant pulpit and in the mood it creates among the faithful. This is all the more shocking since it did not really belong there in the first place.

We have seen that the assumptions of Old Testament worship were theocentric. Worship celebrated his rule and redemption. He made the sun rise and set and gave rain to the parched earth. He overcame the tyrant and led his people through the wilderness. Man's weakness and predetermined fate were transformed into freedom and destiny by the action of God. The experience-centered worship of much of Protestant Christianity is increasingly frustrated because under the impact of the present somber cultural mood, those who participate in it have increasingly grave doubts about man's power to work out his true destiny, even with his Christian "experience." It all seems unrealistic and leads to cynicism.

The recovery of theocentric worship that proclaims the action of God as the basis of man's destiny and the hope of his eschatological redemption could quicken in Christians today a new rationale for their commitment to responsible action in history.

It would also result in a recovery of the meaning of God as Creator, and so provide the basis for an alternative to secularism. Finally, the proclamation of the

Old Testament that God is One both as Creator and
Redeemer can lead to a recovery of the notions of
election and of prevenient grace; which assume a universality in the action of God that experience-centered
worship has lost. And such recovery can become the
beginning of the biblical confession of the Church as
the people of God, a community as universal in time
and space as the action of God itself. The individual
today suffers from estrangement and loneliness even
when he talks about "religious experience." This can
be overcome only when his participation in the worship of the *One* God makes him aware that he belongs
to "an eternal people."

FRANKLIN W. YOUNG

The Theological Context
of New Testament Worship

In this essay I wish to examine the following thesis: there was implicit in Christian theology from the beginning a resistance to any tendency toward defining worship in the narrow sense of cultic rites. Obviously, I do not mean there were no cultic rites. Rather, I mean that the worship of the Church as popularly conceived after almost 2000 years of history does not do justice to the theological context in which the early Church understood its worship. Worship, conceived as the joyful response of Christians to God's action in Jesus Christ, was not defined first and foremost in terms of what happened in a certain *place where* and at a certain *time when* Christians assembled. What happened on these occasions was understood within the context of response to God in their total existence.

By implication, then, where this context of understanding prevailed, the New Testament Church did not have such a problem as arises in our day — the problem of endeavoring to see the relation between the worship of the Church, the mission of the Church, and the ethical life of the Church. These were not compartmentalized areas and activities of life, theologically speaking; they were different aspects of the one relation between God and his people. For this reason one does not find in the New Testament a vocabulary of worship in the narrow sense of that word; worship in this bifurcated sense had no separate existence and hence no peculiar vocabulary. It is the purpose of this paper to examine the basis in the New Testament for these claims which may seem strange or excessive.

I

It is an historical fact that the New Testament Church had no *holy place*, spatially located, which could be designated as *the place* where God, in some special sense, was present to his people. As a religious community the Christians were in this respect atypical in the Graeco-Roman world. Their situation contrasted with that of Judaism with its temple in Jerusalem and the synagogues throughout the Diaspora. The growing significance of the Synagogue, from the theological standpoint, did not minimize the importance of the Temple so long as it stood. It was called *the place* already in the Old Testament. It would obviously be wrong to limit God's presence crudely to the Temple;

but it would be just as erroneous to fail to recognize the Temple's peculiar significance as the place where God had chosen to meet his people. And if there were crucial differences in theological understanding between Judaism and contemporary pagan religions, nevertheless, they too had temples and shrines which were peculiarly sacred to the gods worshipped there. They had their *holy places*. In contrast with both Judaism and Graeco-Roman religious cults the early Christian Church had no *holy place* or *places* which had been peculiarly chosen by God as his place of visitation. Jews could speak of going up to the Temple, or God's house, or the synagogue. Pagans could likewise speak of going to the temple or the shrine. The phrase "going to church" is an impossible linguistic construction in the New Testament.

If we think of worship in the narrow cultic sense, the Christians had no *place of worship*. More than that, they had nothing to do that could be called worship in the cultic sense. There was no *holy place* uniquely related to the presence of God where what took place (worship) was crucially significant for the continuing relationship between God and his people. In this sense also the Christian situation contrasted from that of Judaism and the pagan cults with their elaborate cultic rituals, which defined the worship carried on in the *holy place* or *places*.

The historical judgment that the early Christians

felt they had no *holy place* must be qualified on grounds of the New Testament itself. As long as the Temple stood there was an element of ambiguity on the part of Jewish Christians in their attitude toward the Temple. It is likely that there were those who continued to worship in the Temple and perhaps in Jewish synagogues as well. Such ambiguities were eliminated by historical events when the Temple was destroyed and the growing conflict between Jews and Christians rendered attendance at synagogue a virtual impossibility.

This might appear to suggest that the peculiar situation of the Christians, without a *holy place* where *holy worship* transpired, was an historical accident. But historical events merely laid bare the theological truth already implicit in a tradition founded upon another event: the life, death, and resurrection of Jesus Christ. Historical events, including the destruction of the Temple and its consequences, played a role in casting Christians adrift from any locus or mode of worship in the narrow sense of the term. However, operative in the mind and tradition of the Church was a theological context of understanding which provided the positive and determinative resistance to the localization and compartmentalization of worship. Historical events merely removed the ambiguity which for a time concealed the full truth of this theological understanding.

II

One important mode of access to the New Testament theological context of worship is consideration of a traditional saying of Jesus. It was the starting point for a very significant theological interpretation. The Synoptics record the saying with only slight variation.

And as he came out of the temple, one of his disciples said to him, "Look, Teacher, what wonderful stones and what wonderful buildings!" And Jesus said to him, "Do you see these great buildings? There will not be left here one stone upon another, that will not be thrown down." (Mark 13:1-2; cp. Matt. 24:1-3; Luke 21:5-6.)

The authenticity of a prophecy uttered by Jesus regarding the destruction of the Temple is further substantiated by one of the accusations at his trial. Fake witnesses say: "We heard him say, I will destroy this temple that is made with hands (*ton naon touton cheiropoieton*) and in three days I will build another, not made with hands" (*acheiropoieton oikodomeso*). This is clearly a garbled version of the above prophecy. The important fact is that it already reflects the theological interpretation of the early Church under the influence of the resurrection faith. We are not primarily concerned here to discuss the mode in which Jesus expected the Temple's destruction (socio-historical or apocalyptic). Our interest is focused on the

New Testament interpretation of Jesus' prophecy as it became one of the important factors in determining the theological context for understanding Christian worship.

It is the Gospel of John which provides the explicit interpretation that is already implicit in the trial saying. More than that, in John the implications for a theological context of Christian worship are brought into sharp focus.

The Johannine version of Jesus' prophecy is found imbedded in the pericope of the cleansing of the Temple (2:13–22). When the Jews ask for a sign to warrant his action, Jesus replies: "Destroy this temple, and in three days I will raise it up." The Jews are unable to understand how this can be. The author informs his readers: "But he spoke of the temple of his body" (*peri tou naou tou somatou*). The Synoptic form of the saying at the trial merely alludes to the death and resurrection. In John, the allusion is to the destruction of the Temple, while the words "you destroy" and "raise up" refer directly to the death and resurrection of Jesus. By locating his version of the saying in the context of the cleansing of the Temple, John means to say that in the death and resurrection of Jesus the Temple of Jerusalem is supplanted as the *place* where God is peculiarly present to his people and the central place of worship. This was for him the hidden meaning of the cleansing of the Temple — the meaning finally disclosed through the death and resurrection of Jesus. There is a new temple, a new place where God is present to his people — the risen Lord. That this is the theological meaning intended by John is further substantiated in the dialogue with the Samaritan woman (ch. 4). When the woman says that the Jews say the place (*topos*) where one must worship is in Jerusalem (4:21), Jesus replies: "Woman, believe me, the hour is coming when neither on this mountain nor in Jerusalem will you worship the Father." This hour in John culminates in the death and resurrection of Jesus Christ. The truth of all that is disclosed in this event awaits the coming of the Spirit (16:12–15). True worshippers (*proskunetai*) are those who worship in Spirit and truth (4:23). Where do such worship? It is just where they confront God in and through the risen Christ — the Temple — through the Holy Spirit.

After describing Jesus' action in the cleansing of the Temple, John reports that his disciples remembered that it was written, "Zeal for thy house will consume me" (2:17; Ps. 69:9). While "house" alludes to the Temple in Jerusalem, it actually symbolizes the presence of God, which is to be uniquely manifest in the death, resurrection, and coming of the Spirit. God presents himself to man in the death which "consumes" Christ, and the resurrection through which Christ becomes the *place* where God and man meet through the Spirit. At the beginning of the chapters dealing

specifically with the Holy Spirit (ch. 14–16) Jesus
says:

> In my father's house are many rooms (*monas*). If it were not
> so I would have told you. I go to prepare a place (*topos*)
> for you and if I go and prepare a place (*topos*) for you, I
> come again and take you to myself, in order that where I
> am you also may be (14:2–3).

The meaning of this passage can be understood only
in the light of the later promise. "If a man loves me,
he will keep my word, and my Father will love him,
and we will come to him and make our home (*monen*)
with him" (14:23). The place (*topos*) is a room
(*mone*) in God's house. But Christ takes the believers
to it only as he comes with the Father and makes his
home with them. Clearly then, the new *place* (*topos*),
or *house* (temple?) of the Christian is where Christ
and the Father confront him. And to be in God's house
is to abide in Jesus Christ through the Holy Spirit.

The true worshipper is he who through faith finds
his *place* of obeisance to be Christ, where God presents
himself to man in Spirit and truth. And his obeisance
has reference to his total faith response to God. This
is made particularly clear in chapter 17, frequently
called Christ's "High Priestly prayer." Whatever the
relation of these words to the historical Jesus, John
writes presupposing the ministry, death and resurrection. The first half of the chapter centers attention on
Christ's glorification of God and God's glorification

of Christ. This mutual glorification is achieved in the death-resurrection of Christ through which God is revealed to man and eternal life is revealed and bestowed upon man. The last part of the chapter deals with Christ's consecration of the believers. This consecration involves a mission into the world where by word and deed of love the Church bears witness to the only true God. In the mission the believers are given the glory which God gave Christ, that is, through them testimony is borne to the only true God (17:22). So it is in the total faith response that the believer is consecrated and the ultimate meaning of union with God is articulated. This is worship in Spirit and truth.

If this is a proper reading of the Gospel of John, it is clear how his theological orientation resists any localizing of the context of worship as well as rendering it impossible to draw a hard line between worship in the cultic sense and the mission or work of the Church.

The metaphor of the temple as the place where believers confront God in Jesus Christ is also found in Paul's writings. Paul writes to the Corinthians: "Do you not know that you are God's temple (*naos*) and that God's Spirit dwells in you? If anyone destroys God's temple, God will destroy him. For God's temple is holy, and that temple you are" (1 Cor. 3:16–17). The "you" in each case is plural; here the temple metaphor is used collectively to designate believers. However, in the Pauline theological context, believers are the temple insofar as the indwelling Spirit of Christ is present to faith. Through the Spirit God presents himself to believers. Theologically, then, it is the presence of the Spirit of Christ which constitutes the temple.

In the context of 1 Corinthians 3 it is clear that Paul is laying particular stress upon the believer's response to God in ethical terms. His use of the temple metaphor is closely related to that of the building (*oikodome*) in 1 Corinthians 3:9. It seems most probable that this is a synonym for temple. The building metaphor stresses the dynamic character of the relationship between God and his people. It emphasizes the tension in the faith situation: At one and the same time believers are a temple insofar as the Spirit dwells in them, and are not yet the temple insofar as in the Spirit they are continually being built up into Christ.

It is significant to observe in the one lengthy passage in the Pauline epistles where cultic worship is described (1 Cor. 12–14), the one term used predominantly is "building up" (*oikodomein*). Whatever other associations this word may have, there is no doubt of its connection with the building-temple metaphor. It is clear that in this passage "building up" cannot be limited to worship in the narrow, cultic sense. For elsewhere Paul uses the word in the strictly ethical sense (1 Cor. 8:1; 10:23; Rom. 14:19; 15:2; 1 Thess. 5:11). In other words, when discussing cultic worship, Paul employs a term which regularly describes the ethical life. And the word he uses derives from the building-temple metaphor, which is for Paul a symbol of the presence of God through the Spirit of Christ.

There is another interesting phenomenon in Paul's letters. He frequently uses traditional Jewish cultic terminology to describe his apostolic activity. For example, he is a minister (*leitourgon*) of Christ Jesus to the Gentiles in the priestly service (*hierourgounta*) of the Gospel of God, so that the offerings (*prosphora*) of the gentiles may be acceptable (*euprosdektos*), consecrated by the Holy Spirit (Rom. 15:16). Paul writes of his ministry to the Philippians: "Even if I am to be poured as a libation (*spendomai*) upon the sacrificial offering (*epi te thusia kai leitourgia*) of your faith, I am glad and rejoice with you all" (Phil. 2:17). And he urges the Romans: "Present your bodies as a living sacrifice (*thusian dyosan*), holy and acceptable to God which is your spiritual worship" (*logiken latreian*, Rom. 12:1). This is a clear exhortation to ethical action as the following verses show. It is the temple metaphor which is behind Paul's choice of cultic terminology to describe this activity. But it does not describe cultic worship in the narrow sense.

This discussion, which began with a saying of Jesus, the Gospel of John and the epistles of Paul, could be extended to other New Testament writings, particularly Ephesians, Hebrews, Revelation, and 1 Peter. Though theological language would vary, the theological implications for the understanding of worship would be the same. They would be consistent with the following conclusions which can be drawn from the above consideration of John and Paul:

(1) By locating the temple or *holy place* at the point where God confronts man in the person of the risen Lord (with respect to God's action) or the Church (with respect to response in faith) the possibility of spatially localizing worship in abstraction from the totality of life was impossible. The *holy place*, from God's side, is as omnipresent as the risen Christ (through the Holy Spirit); and, from man's side, it is co-extensive with the faith-response to God's act in Christ.

(2) This resulted in a radically new theological context for understanding worship. There was clearly a sense in which any response in faith could be thought of in terms of worship — the encounter with God in his chosen place. Thus the mission of the Church conceived in terms of its proclamation in word and deed was inextricably bound to its cultic worship. This frustrated any tendency to understand worship as an autonomous inturned activity.

(3) By the utilization of traditional cultic terms when speaking of aspects of its life which in no sense were

cultic, the early Church reflects its own awareness of the radical new context in which its worship was to be understood. However, the crucial fact was not the new use of words but the decisive event which gave the words their radical new context of meaning. That event was God's act in Jesus Christ's life, death, and resurrection.

(4) Insofar as worship, in the cultic sense, was seen within this larger context it pointed away from itself to that decisive event. It pointed to the event which shattered all possibility of localizing God's presence, of isolating worship and confining it within the bonds of traditional and technical vocabulary and forms. Worship had a new center, vocabulary, and form — Jesus Christ.

III

Recent scholarship has repeatedly underscored the fact that the New Testament refrains from using traditional cultic terminology (e.g. *latreia, leitourgia, diakonia,* etc.) to refer to its cultic worship. The importance of this cannot be overemphasized. There must have been a good reason. I should like to suggest that a principal reason was the Church's conviction that, even as God's holy place of meeting men was disclosed in Jesus Christ, so Jesus Christ's action was determinative for the meaning of worship. At the risk of misunderstanding let me overstate the case. In the cultic sense the early Christians had nothing to do to worship. Unlike the Jews with their cultic service (*latreia, leitourgia*) well defined by Torah, the Christians had none. What they were to do in response to God, Christ had done. Or to put it another way: the true worship of God was disclosed in Christ's action. Their attention was focused on Christ's service.

This concentration on Christ's service had important consequences. Any possibility of a division between "worship" and "work" was precluded by the fact that Christ's service was seen in terms of the whole deed of Christ (or God in Christ). Christ's obedience (obeisance) was seen in terms of his total ministry, his words, his deeds, his death, his resurrection, his session at the right hand of God, his coming again. Worship meant responding to that total deed of Christ in one's total existence. Worship was understood not primarily from the standpoint of what *man* does, but from the standpoint of response to what Christ did and was continuing to do. Since Christ's continuing action was seen in terms of this total response in the world, traditional terms that would suggest restricting the response of "worship" to cultic acts alone were transformed to describe their total response to Christ.

It is at this point that a qualification must be placed upon the statement that in the cultic sense of worship the Christians had nothing to do. For in the total deed of Christ were the words which instituted the Lord's

Supper. However, the Lord's Supper itself pointed away from itself, beyond the words of the Last Supper, to the very event which shattered all possibility of localizing God's presence, Christ's presence, and of isolating worship.

Why is this so? Whether we see the Lord's Supper as the meal anticipating the joyous Messianic feast, or the proclamation of Christ's death, or the participation in the life of the risen Lord, or a combination of these, it points beyond itself to the action of the Lord. Whatever else must be said regarding the "subjective" meaning of the Lord's Supper to Christians, it is said within the context of the death and resurrection which occurred "there" and the coming "then." The celebration of the Lord's Supper as a "now" of the death, resurrection, and coming, therefore, points away to a once-for-all "there" of the death and resurrection and a "then" of the crucified-risen Lord's coming. However one interprets the presence in the Lord's Supper of the crucified-risen-coming Lord, both the death-resurrection event and the coming event, in some real sense, stand over against and determine the meaning that constitutes the celebration of the Lord's Supper. It pointed away from itself to this decisive, complex event, and was celebrated as a "moment" whose content and meaning were utterly dependent upon this event and the Lord of that event.

What is being suggested is that the very cultic rite

which was at the center of the early Church's worship
shattered the possibility of conceiving of worship adequately in traditional cultic terms and forms. This must
be understood both historically and theologically. The
Christians had no "holy place," spatially conceived, to
celebrate the Lord's Supper. There was no designated
"place," sanctuary, altar, holy of holies, within the
confines of which they knew their Lord would present himself. Any "house" where a "table" was spread
might become "a place" where the crucified-risen-
coming Lord might be received, known, proclaimed
in breaking bread. The very fact that the Eucharist
could occur "any place" bore witness to the truth
that the Lord's presence could not be "localized" in
any place. The Lord who made "any place" his place
in Eucharist was the same Lord who made "any place"
his place, where in faith's hearing of the Word worshipful response was possible. The "house" or "place"
where Eucharist was held was "in the world," hal-
lowed in the moment of Christ's coming to the faithful.
It was the same house or place in the world made
holy by Christ's coming to those who heard the Word.
The "place" of the Eucharist and the "place" of the
mission were one and the same place — the world —
and any place in that world where in faith Christians
broke bread or responded to the Word in word and
deed. The Eucharist itself, as worship, bore witness
to the impossibility of understanding worship from

any other standpoint than the response of the believer in the totality of his life in the world.

There is one other point to be made in explicating the claim that the Eucharist shattered the possibility of conceiving of worship adequately in traditional cultic terms and forms. Let me discuss this by drawing a contrast. In religious rites of Hellenistic cults the adherence to exact technical religious formulae and liturgies was necessary. This was true because the principal actors in the cult rites were the devotees. In pagan cults based on rationalized myths it was the hierophant and the devotees who were the central actors. Of necessity there was preoccupation with what was done liturgically, and the necessity of correct action. While the theological understanding of the actions differed vastly in Judaism, nevertheless, the minute descriptions for clergy and people regulating the Temple cultus gave weighty attention to the action of the people and the liturgical structure of that action. In spite of the vast theological chasm between Jewish Temple worship and pagan cults, in both instances cultic worship was peculiarly related to and defined by these special actions.

In the Lord's Supper, the primary actor was the Lord, crucified-risen-coming. This involved a significant shift of emphasis from the believer, as the center of action and worship, to Christ as the center of action and worship. The very diversities in the New Testa-

ment traditions of the Lord's Supper point to a break
from traditional religion, in the Church's lack of preoccupation with exact language and action (formally
speaking). The words of institution, varied though
they be, pointed to that event which could not finally
be reduced or sanctified or captured by words about
that event. My point is not to deny that there were
words which already suggest liturgy in the narrow
sense. It is merely to emphasize that the overwhelming
awareness of the Lord as actor transformed the understanding and place of language and action of those
sharing in the Eucharist. Their concern was not to define cultic worship from the standpoint of human action, but to enter into the only perfect act of worship,
that of Jesus Christ. That act constituted the Lord's
Supper, and their participation was an act of faith
in response to it.

What was new in Christian worship was constituted
by the new thing God had done in Jesus Christ. The
Lord's Supper proclaimed this. If with the synagogue
they read and expounded the Holy Scriptures, prayed
and chanted psalms, it all occurred not far from the
"table" where they celebrated the revelation of God
that provided the theological context for their understanding of true worship. As the "table" might appear
anywhere in the world, so the deed of the Lord might
encounter man anywhere in the world. As the Lord

of the Table had disclosed true worship in the total
obedience of his life, so true worship was entrance into
his obedience wherever and whenever the faithful lived
out their lives in encounter with his deed. This is the
theological context of understanding worship which
from the beginning is behind the apparent resistance
in the New Testament to any tendency toward defining worship in the narrow sense of cultic rites.

IV

If there is any validity in this interpretation of the
theological context of New Testament worship, what
does it say in the present to the Church as it seeks to
understand its worship and express its faith through
worship? Above all, it would focus its thought regarding worship on Jesus Christ. It would be oriented in
the faith that in Jesus Christ alone the true worship of
God is disclosed. And it would understand this worship in terms of his total life, death, resurrection, session at the right hand of God, coming again, seen as
the perfect obedience to God and communion with
God. It would understand its own worship as participation in Christ's worship. And it would understand
its derivative worship theologically in the context of
its total life in the world — a world which at any place
and time might become the holy place where the grace
of Christ's obedience is bestowed, and where the sum-

mons to share in Christ's obedience is responsively received.

Such a focus of attention would not by some miracle dissolve all issues. It would provide a context of understanding which might create a new mind for appraising, and a new heart for resolving, important issues. It would certainly challenge any compartmentalization of worship which separates it from work and mission. An inescapable question mark would be placed against any tendencies to conceive of cultic worship primarily from the standpoint of man's action. And the shadow of that question mark would hover over the traditional modes of worship insofar as they become areas of dispute by overemphasizing, consciously or unconsciously, man's action as the center of attention in Christian worship.

In calling the Church to the remembrance that the *leitourgia, latreia,* and *diakonia* belong to Christ, that is, that they derive from and are constituted by his person and work, the Church would be challenged. This would occur primarily at that point where it spoke of "our worship," especially when such language frustrates the call to the one worship of and through Jesus Christ. Set loose from the indifference or tenacity toward "our worship" by the claims of Christ's one worship, the mind of the faithful might be prepared to receive from the author of all worship a mode and manner of worship. If so, it would be a

leitourgia whereby the one worship might be manifested in all the world through the earthen vessel of
an emerging historical tradition.

And what about the Table of the Lord? If the faithful were to see the Table of the Lord as the celebration of the event which called all traditions of worship
into question, they might be summoned to come to
the Table, submitting to that question, in the faith
that the Lord of the Table will provide the way to
celebrate, rather than to question, that event.

The Norm and Freedom
of Christian Worship

In order to understand the worship of the Church it must be viewed in its relationship to the author of the Christian faith. Two assumptions can easily color the concept of Christian worship and distort it. In popular terms worship is usually understood as "paying divine honors to a deity" (Webster). By applying this concept to a particular religion, one is inclined to define worship in terms of cultus only. With respect to Christianity this might mean analyzing how the Lord's Supper became the Sunday Eucharist, a ceremonial rather than a meal. Or, Baptism might be studied as initiatory rite of the Church. The most effective way of avoiding a myopic view of Christian worship in terms of cultus is to relate its origin to Jesus Christ.

The other assumption that can also contribute to a narrow view of Christian worship regards it as service of God in various deeds of commitment without immediate cultic implications: visiting the widows and the fatherless, for example. Cultic acts, such as the breaking of the bread, from this point of view are considered meaningful only as part of the practical *leitourgia* or *diakonia*.

In the New Testament, however, the cultic and the ethical aspects of worship are not exclusive of each other. There is a tendency toward the complete abandonment of cultus as well as a development of new cultic expressions. The temple in Jerusalem is replaced by a new temple, the body of Jesus, (John 2: 21); or God together with the Lamb is thought of as new temple (Rev. 21:22). Jesus as the Christ is spoken of as high priest (Heb. 9:11). Circumcision becomes a matter of the heart (Rom. 2:29). The transformation of cultic forms and concepts indicated in these few examples, on the one hand, points to a movement away from cultus. The Lord's Supper and Baptism, on the other hand, prove that there was no general rejection of cultic expressions.

The transformation of old cultic forms and concepts and the development of new rites in the Church cannot be understood as a complete accident of history. It is partly due to the nature of man. Cultus is not an absolutely necessary requirement for man's well-being, but an inevitable expression of his predicament. Paul Tillich articulates the inevitability of cultus rather well: "There should be neither myth nor cult. They contradict essential reason; they betray by their very existence the 'fallen' state of a reason which has lost immediate unity with its own depth. It has become 'superficial,' cutting itself off from its ground and abyss." [1] There should be no cult!

The early Church understood the tentative character of cult rather well: "The hour is coming when neither on this mountain nor in Jerusalem will you worship the Father. . . . The hour is coming, and now is, when the true worshippers will worship the Father in spirit and truth." (John 4:21, 23) As much as early Christianity saw the tentativeness of cult, it could not escape the human condition. What it regarded as complete victory over the human predicament, it also expressed in cultic symbols that partook of the predicament. The forms of the Christian cultus are not perfect or ideal means of communicating the Christian truth. They are tentative arrangements of a people that is trying more and more fully to grasp the basic datum of its ultimate commitment. But they proved unavoidable from the very beginning. The same Gospel that speaks of the totally spiritual worship also refers to the water of baptism (John 3:5), as well as to the eating of the flesh of the Son of Man and the drinking of his blood (John 6:53). Even if it had been the redactor that introduced these references into the Fourth Gospel, they none the less would show also that Christianity could not escape cultic expression.

The enlightenment thought it could dispense entirely with cultic worship. Immanuel Kant, for example, took man to task for his stupidity in continuing to share in rites that have no relevance. Of worship he said: "Whatever, over and above good life-conduct, man fancies that he can do to become well-pleasing to God is mere religious illusion and pseudo-service of God." [2] Kant's position implied that man performs God's commands by fulfilling his duty toward his fellowman, and that it is absolutely impossible to serve God more directly, since men supposedly affect and have influence upon earthly beings alone. Kant presupposed also that Christian worship is an attempt of man to become *well-pleasing* to God. He lacked sensitivity for other possibilities of interpreting Christian worship. The difficulty is aggravated by his nonchalant view of the central datum of the Christian faith: "It must be inculcated painstakingly and repeatedly that true religion is to consist not in the knowing or considering of what God does or has done for our salvation but in what we must do to become worthy of it." [3] It would be ideal to live in such a state as envisioned by Kant. In any case, it would make the present essay superfluous.

What Kant overlooked is that man has rejected his

true being and is ignorant of the source of his life and its ultimate meaning. Man is taken too seriously with respect to his religious or moral ability and finally thrown into despair, since he cannot come to grips with the meaning of his life by his own effort. The concomitant of debunking Christian worship is the forgetfulness of God, of what he has done and still does. A neglect of worship implies an unawareness of God's claim that man acknowledge his deeds. Kant represents the attack of modern man upon the Christian view of man's nature. Anything we say of Christian worship must keep this nonchalant stance of modern man in mind. But an equally important misunderstanding of Christian worship is found in the Church itself, insofar as it misconstrues in the spiritual beauty-culture of a Sallman-Jesus what God has done and still does.

I   CHRISTIAN WORSHIP AND GOD'S BEING

What is the Christian doing in the act of worship? He certainly intends to acknowledge God. But how can he acknowledge a God who is not directly available to him? In worship the Christian ventures to recapitulate those events in which God's being has been acknowledged in its true character. He tries to recapture what God is like in what God has done and still does. It is not only in worship that the Christian makes this effort. The entire life of the Church is involved — evangelism, works of love, etc. Theology as an effort of the Church is also an attempt at recapturing the character of God's deeds. The new quest of the historical Jesus as a specific theological effort, to use a contemporary example, can be meaningful only as it shares in this basic attempt of theology. Hugh Anderson describes the situation succinctly:

Encounter with the Christ is not . . . to be confined to the climactic experience of an isolated moment in time. It is rather the continual recapitulating, re-enacting and re-living of the history of Jesus the Christ, in which the members of the Church in fellowship together are regular participators. This is best illustrated from an appeal to liturgy. . . . The liturgy of the Christian Church calls us to the realization of fellowship with Jesus Christ through participation in the Christ-deed in the totality of its meaning as the redemptive action of God. . . . The liturgy, which is the very essence of the Church's life, perpetuates the Kerygma's fusion of the humiliated and crucified with the risen and exalted Lord. The Church therefore can never dispense with the historical Jesus.[4]

Unmistakably Christian worship points to Jesus of Nazareth.[5] But in what sense is Christian worship interested in him? It proceeds with the conviction that God's plan and purpose hinges completely on his deed in Jesus. Joseph Sittler has claimed that interest in the deed means concern for the shape of the deed:

To be a Christian is to have one's life in its shape determined by the shape of what God has done. . . . The morphology of grace in the life, death, resurrection, and exaltation of Jesus Christ imparts to and creates in the believer its own shape — so worship is the celebration of this new being in Christ by his body, the church. . . . As then we . . . observe how this shape, re-enacted within the behavior by the power of the Holy Spirit, constituted Christian life in the fellowship of the community, do we not also, perhaps, find a pattern for Christian worship? . . . If that is so, then we are given a starting place where, from within our various churches we ask after what is constitutive of and proper to the content of truly catholic worship.[6]

The shape of God's deed shapes the believer's life. Christian worship in this respect is the corporate attempt of Christians to remember and to embody the shape of God's deed in order to rehearse and to strengthen the life of the individual believer.

What is still in question is what Sittler presupposes: the *shape* of the deed of God. What exactly is the shape of Jesus' life, death and resurrection? The New Testament was concerned to present the shape. But it did not present it in a perfect copy or photograph. It interpreted it. Part of the interpretation took place in Christian worship. Thus God's being in the shape of his deed is available to us only in the witness of the New Testament. It raises the question whether the interpretation properly grasped the deed of God. In order to get a more comprehensive view of the question we turn to one of the New Testament writings, the Fourth Gospel.

II THE FOURTH GOSPEL AND CHRISTIAN WORSHIP

Oscar Cullmann has introduced the thesis that the Fourth Gospel is permeated by references to Christian worship, especially Baptism and the Lord's Supper; not in every passage, but frequently enough that one should take special note of it. For example, the wine miracle (2:1–11) points to the Lord's Supper. The conversation with Nicodemus (3:1–21) refers to Baptism, as well as the healing of the man born blind (9:1–39). Also in the washing of the disciples' feet (13:1–20) Cullmann finds a reference to Baptism. The most comprehensive references to the Lord's Supper he discovers, of course, in the feeding of the five thousand with its discourse sequel (6:1–13, 26–65). There are other references Cullmann considers important. As illustration may serve 19:34, the verse on the spear-thrust which, in Cullmann's words, "contains the key to the understanding of the passages we have examined." [7]

Water and blood flowed from Jesus' side because of the soldier's spear-thrust. The water and blood respectively point to Baptism and the Lord's Supper: "Scarcely is the historical Jesus dead — his body still hangs upon the Cross — when he shows in what form he will from now on be present upon earth, in the sacraments, in Baptism and Lord's Supper, and we know from chapter 6 that this presence is just as real as the water and the blood from his wounds were real." [8] The way Cullmann sees Jesus introduce his presence in the Church borders upon the mythological. But Cullmann does accomplish one thing in concentrating on the references to Baptism and the Lord's Supper in the Fourth Gospel: he clearly shows that the theology of the early Church, in trying to understand the earthly Jesus, was immersed in what was taking place in its life of worship. In what sense the Jesus who died shows how he will be present in the sacraments is a question to which we return later.

Cullmann rightly sees that the Fourth Gospel is an interpretation of the Jesus of history under the guidance of the Holy Spirit, as the references to the Paraclete indicate (cf. 14:26 and 16:12f). The real meaning of Jesus' ministry has been ascertained only after Jesus' death and resurrection. The author of the Fourth Gospel has written in the "consciousness of being inspired by the Paraclete." [9] He remembers certain facts, but this memory is "not merely a remembering of the material facts, it includes alongside this that understanding of the facts which is first granted through the Holy Spirit." [10] This is certainly not an inappropriate view of what happens in the theologizing of the Fourth Gospel. But in turning our attention to the understanding effected by the Holy Spirit we dare not neglect the inquiry concerned with the data which the Holy Spirit interprets. Cullmann knows that the interest in the sacraments is only one aspect of the concern of the Fourth Gospel, which is "to set forth the line from the life of Jesus to the Christ of the community, in such a way as to demonstrate their identity." [11] For Cullmann this implies an analysis of the Christ in his significance for the community. But it is not quite clear that this also involves how "the historical Jesus corresponds to the Christ of the Church." [12] In the evangelist's mind "the life of Jesus is always based on a conspectus of the historical Jesus and the Lord present in the community." [13] The Lord who is present in the community stands out quite clearly in Cullmann, but not the historical Jesus.

This does not mean to suggest that Cullmann is completely uninterested in the actual life of Jesus, as the following review of his understanding of the relationship between Jesus and the sacraments will show. But his view of the relationship is uncritical. "It is the person of Jesus, not the baptizing, that is first set over against the baptizing of John." [14] Jesus was baptized "to undertake the rôle of the servant of God, suffering vicariously for his people." [15] His baptism was "for the benefit of all and which therefore makes the baptism of John superfluous." [16] Cullmann is interested at this point in emphasizing that the Fourth Gospel "indirectly bears witness to the conception of Christian Baptism as a Baptism into the death of Christ corresponding to the Pauline teaching in Romans 6." [17]

As regards the Lord's Supper, we mentioned before that Cullmann already regards the wine miracle as pointing to the holy meal. He states: "When we take into account the fact that the Cana story is regarded as *a pointer to the death of Christ* because of the word about the hour that is not yet come, and when we take into account further that in chapter 6 the bread is connected with the bread of the Last Supper, it seems a most likely explanation that the wine points to the blood of Christ offered in the Lord's Supper." [18] What have we learned if we know that the wine at the wedding points to the death of Jesus and to the blood that is symbolized in the Lord's Supper? According to Cullman, the following: "Clearly the sacraments mean the same for the Church as the miracles of the historical Jesus for his contemporaries." [19]

Cullmann rightly understands that the centrally important fact in the Fourth Gospel is Jesus who replaces the temple; Jesus Christ has become the center of worship. But he concentrates too much on the sacraments. It is true that "the media of the past which sought to restore the bond of unity between God and sinful man (purificatory rites, washings, baptism of John), are replaced by the media of grace," [20] the sacraments. It is more important, however, to stress that the media of the past are first of all replaced by the person of Jesus of Nazareth. This is what the author of the Fourth Gospel, especially under the influence of his anti-docetic concern, wants to stress. The sacraments, as much as they might have been in the mind of the author, are not even explicitly mentioned. Whatever might be sacramentally colored in the Fourth Gospel points to a basic demand: the reader is asked to make a decision relative to Jesus. The author himself wants to say more fully who Jesus is. Basic to this "more fully" is the relationship of God to this man Jesus. The author sees Jesus more in the context of history, the movement from baptism to the Cross, than from the viewpoint of sacramental worship. The death of Jesus is part of a thorny road God himself walked together with his Son. The interconnections between worship and the public ministry of Jesus exist. But they are relevant not so much for proving that the sacraments take the place of Jesus' miracles, as for raising the question: How much did worship itself contribute to the formation of the history of Jesus as told in the Gospels? [21]

III   THE PASSION NARRATIVE AND CHRISTIAN WORSHIP

Cullmann's key idea, John 19:34, is lodged within the Passion narrative. In order to come closer to the shape of Jesus' life we consider separately this body of ma-

terial which is more coherent and uniform as compared with the other parts of the Gospels. The Fourth
Gospel follows the incidents of the Passion quite faith-
fully in contrast to its rather free handling of the pre-
Passion narrative.

Martin Dibelius, in *Die Formgeschichte des Evangeliums*, emphasizes that we must regard the Passion
narrative as the only part of the tradition which, early
in its formation, related incidents in a broader context.
Its form is even older than its composition in Mark's
Gospel.

According to Dibelius the Passion narrative can be
understood only in the light of the Easter experiences
of the disciples. What happened in Jerusalem had
been so revolting that any account of it could only be
looked upon as a document of *shame*. Only if one was
persuaded that Christ lived with the Father and that
the shame and death had come about according to his
will, could one meaningfully report the incident. All
who confessed the resurrected one knew that God's
will had taken place in this obnoxious event.

Scripture proof was not immediately adduced at
this stage. Dibelius believes that it was first only a
postulate of the Easter faith. The Scripture proof rationale developed gradually as follows: Jesus' suffering took place according to God's will; and God's will
must be found in Holy Scripture. Psalms 22, 31, and

69 and Isaiah 53 were passages which seemed to describe the suffering *beforehand*. Certain motifs of these passages entered into the Passion narrative. The dividing of garments, for example, was told according to Psalm 22:18. The offer of vinegar to the dying Jesus reminds one of Psalm 69:21, the mocking of the crucified of Psalm 22:7. Regardless of how many passages could be added (Dibelius cites a considerable number), the important issue is whether the Passion narrative is historical. Some incidents, says Dibelius, may have been read into it on the basis of Old Testament study. For example, the thirty pieces of silver in Matthew 26:15 relate back to Zechariah 11:12. Nevertheless, large portions of the narrative have to be regarded as historical. What the early Church did, however, was to view the historical event of a gruesome crucifixion in the light of the Old Testament in order to find meaning in it.[22]

Mark did not alter much of the oldest account. One change he made was to preface the report of the Last Supper with an introductory legend, which converts it into a Paschal meal. This has no literary reason. It is cultic influence. There were congregations that celebrated the Lord's Supper as continuation of the Paschal meal.[23] Bultmann conjectures that this concept of the Lord's Supper may depend on the Jewish Christian community, which was trying to sanction its con-

tinuance of the old Paschal customs.[24] He believes
one might well ask whether the Fourth Gospel contains the more original account of the supper.[25]

Proclamation and cultus influenced the understanding of the historical events. The Christian viewed
them in terms of a history of salvation. Besides the
mere historical report on certain facts of the Passion
story, the "creative" interpretation of the early Christian community is part of the picture. This cannot be
understood as an attempt to glamorize the corporate
worship of the early community, but as an effort to
find divine meaning in what externally could only be
regarded as a failure. Before developing any compli-
cated doctrine of the Christian cultus, one should try
to recapture the utter defeat of the man from Nazareth and the crude shape of the events that lie behind
the theological reflection of the early Church. Very
little can be ascertained with objective certainty of
the history of Jesus. This is especially true of what we
have referred to as the shape of his ministry.[26] But
what can be ascertained is his utter humiliation, to
which the more or less incoherent accounts of his
ministry and death bear witness.

The result of our study thus far has been rather
negative. All we were able to say of worship was that
it is faith-interpretation of a history that is not fully
available to us in all its concrete aspects, its causal
sequence, or chronology. But this is important to re-

member in view of much that passes for Christian worship in our time, from the triumph of electronic organs to the glory of switchboards that render proper lighting effects for accommodating every whim and mood of a worshipping congregation. The Gospel accounts can teach us that Christian worship pertains to a crude human story, a life of humiliation and revolting defeat. It is regrettable that Cullmann's analysis of early Christian worship does not penetrate that far "behind" the texts to make this clear. Perhaps his concentration on a single Gospel account misleads us to assume that the passage from the author of the Christian movement to Christian worship is as smooth as the texts would seem to indicate.

Everything that one would like to say about worship becomes less easy if one understands that the shape of Jesus' ministry is itself partly theological interpretation. Proclamation, teaching and, last not least, worship contributed to the making of what we consider today to be the shape of Jesus' public ministry. There is no point to saying that the scarcely dead Jesus showed how he would be present in the sacraments (Cullmann), unless one acknowledges that in such an incident the cultic interpretation of the Church is at work. The claim that the sacraments are to the Church what the miracles of the earthly Jesus were for his contemporaries (Cullmann), disregards an important consideration. Jesus, the worker of miracles, did not succeed in the end. In the sacraments as well as in other manifestations of its life the Church sought to grasp the meaning of his unsuccessful ministry. This seeking of meaning in meaninglessness must be the focus of any theological reflection on Christian worship.

IV   THE UNCRITICAL VIEW OF CHRISTIAN WORSHIP

Our study objects to what might be called, for want of a better word, the uncritical view of worship. The presupposition of many theories of Christian worship is that worship is usually a good thing, that Christian worship is an especially good sort of the usually good thing, that in some respects Christian worship is unique and surpasses less-developed "pagan" forms of worship, and that man better make use of the good thing lest he miss out on one of the thrills of his life. Evelyn Underhill's *Worship* may serve as illustration. A beautifully written book, it also shows considerable scholarly acumen. Only in rare moments, however, does it seem to catch sight of the attempt of the early Church to find meaning in meaninglessness. It usually hovers over the elated and lofty, the artistic and especially the poetic:

Liturgical worship shares with all ritual action the character of *a work of art*. Entering upon it, we leave the lower realism of daily life for the higher realism of a successive action which expresses and interprets eternal truth by the deliberate use of poetic and symbolic material. . . . Since its main function is to suggest the Supernatural and lead men out to communion with the Supernatural, it is by the *methods of poetry* that its chief work will be done." [27]

Underhill does know of the "shamefulness of the cross," [28] but she shows little grasp of what that might have meant historically and quickly turns to embellishing it with poetry.

The basic difficulty with such a view of worship begins with the definition: "Worship, in all its grades and kinds, is the response of the creature to the Eternal." [29] Underhill says much of Christian worship in particular. But whatever she describes is pressed into the framework of the general definition of worship. In order to understand what Christian worship is, one should immediately begin considering its specific aspects and the critical light it throws on religion-in-general and worship-in-general or "humanity's universal instinct to worship." [30] If one turns to the specific with the general rule of thumb that the transcendent god *must* be embodied, one stays in the realm of generalities.[31] In Underhill's book the obnoxiousness of Jesus' life and death is immediately made subject to a neat theological formula which admits of no real problem: "the historical embodies the metaphysical, and presents the deep mysteries of Eternal Life to us in a way that we can apprehend." [32]

Man must use images to grasp the embodiment of the metaphysical. They are all inadequate, however, since no man has seen God. It should be clear in this context that Scripture does not say, "No man has seen God, the images reveal him." It says that it is the Son who reveals him. As long as one thinks of Christian worship in terms of worship in general, one will always be quick to stress the importance of art and its images: "The soul in this world passes its life among pictures." [33] Much time will be spent on asking which pictures are the most effective to create a worshipful mood without reflecting on what it actually is that the pictures of Christian worship are to image. The greatest creations of Christian liturgy — for example, the Eucharistic liturgy — are then viewed as "sacred dramas, in which the mystery of salvation is re-enacted and re-experienced by the worshipping group." [34] We agree, of course, that man is an image-making being. But what is "the mystery of salvation"? Is it obvious to the average worshipper? The following general tenet immediately should be subjected to this question: "It is only by recourse to our image-making faculty, or by some reference — direct or oblique — to the things that are seen, that we can ever give concrete form to our intuition of that which is unseen." [35] Man's image-making faculty, as applied to the Christian cultus, must be examined in the light of the basic

Christian datum, the defeat of the man from Nazareth on the Cross.

Underhill affirms that Jesus Christ is our sacrament.[36] In him all image-making has found a focus. She also sees that certain events in Jesus' life are central to the Christian understanding of worship: "In the three crucial events of the Passion — the Last Supper, Gethsemane, and the Cross — the deepest and most awful meanings of the sacrifice of communion, of total oblation, and of atonement, are declared." [37] In view of the full lowliness of God, Underhill can admit: "Christian attempts at a splendour and beauty which shall incarnate something of our reverent delight in the splendour and beauty of God, and witness to His penetration of time and space, must be balanced by at least an equal recognition of *the bareness and humility* through which His approach was made to us." [38] But does Underhill understand that the splendor and beauty of God *is* his bareness and humility on the Cross? Instead of really facing the question of the bareness and humility of God, Underhill almost immediately is absorbed in the totality of worship needs: "Christian worship in its fulness should include and harmonize all the various phases of our human experience. It has room for the extremes of awestruck adoration and penitent love, humble demand and inward assurance. All levels of life and action are relevant to

it, for they are covered and sanctified by the principle
of incarnation." [39] What is questionable in her view
is that God's humiliation is introduced as balancing his
splendor. Thus "awestruck adoration" is isolated from
the Cross, the basic datum of the Christian faith. "Awestruck adoration and penitent love, humble demand
and inward assurance" must be informed by the basic
datum. Otherwise there is no point to them in the
context of Christian worship. Since Underhill fum-
bles on this score, we believe that her view is an ex-
emplary specimen of the uncritical view of Christian
worship.

V   CHRISTIAN WORSHIP IN THE LIGHT OF THE
    CENTRAL CHRISTIAN DATUM

The validity and meaningfulness of Christian liturgy
in America today is taken too much for granted. The
valiant efforts that liturgical churches at the present
time are making to recapture the true spirit of the
liturgy are moving and by no means superfluous.[40]
But the question remains whether they really get at
the heart of the matter and help the worshipper understand who the God is whom he worships. Underhill is
right that there is a double orientation of worship: to
God transcendent and to God incarnate. "This double orientation to the natural and the supernatural,
testifying at once to the unspeakable otherness of

God transcendent and the intimate nearness of God incarnate, is felt in all the various expressions of genuine Christian worship." [41] But God transcendent has to be more understood in terms of God incarnate than God incarnate has to be grasped as God transcendent. The God we are invited to glorify in worship is the God who is lowly, and who is not ashamed of an obscure manger and an obnoxious cross. But we do not quite understand what this means for worship as long as we do not fully face the crude shape of God's deed in Jesus. Worship must be part of the total effort of Christian life to grasp the deed of God. This is especially necessary in the context of American culture-religion. Says Peter L. Berger:

It is difficult to imagine how the religiously mature, socially respectable, and psychologically adjusted church member in our situation can come to terms with the naked horror of Calvary or the blazing glory of Easter morning. Both his religion and his culture compel him to sentimentalize, neutralize, assimilate these Christian images. If he did not do so, they would challenge his religiosity and his respectability and might even threaten his so-called mental health.[42]

We can speak of worship in pragmatic terms only with reference to the *norm* by which we can measure the meaning of genuflection, antiphonal responses, candles, and incense. The fact that it is difficult to ascertain in its specific form adds an additional incentive to being modest about the adequacy of our litur-

gical forms. The realization that the norm of the liturgy is still not fully known means that we cannot
speak of the shape of the liturgy in quite certain terms.
As our understanding of the shape of God's deed is
still growing, the shape of the liturgy is still evolving.
Of course, we cannot indefinitely postpone worshipping because of our ignorance of the true shape of
God's deed. We must worship in tentative patterns.
The least we can do, however, is so to restructure them
that the celebration of God's triumph in lowliness is
not repressed by the hallelujahs of our self-congratula-
tion. Worship that does not confront us with "the
naked horror of Calvary" is spiritual self-adulation
that will never grasp "the blazing glory of the Easter
morning." It has nothing to do with the glorification
of the true God.

The thesis of this paper finds support in a recent
publication of Günther Bornkamm's in *Evangelische
Theologie*, "Geschichte und Glaube im Neuen Testament." [43] Referring to the Arnoldshain theses on the
Lord's Supper, he especially lifts out the first one:
"The Supper which we celebrate is founded in the institution and in the order of Jesus Christ, the Lord,
who was delivered unto death for us and who rose."
The thesis was cautiously formulated without a reference to an historical datum. It does not, for example,
say: "Jesus Christ instituted the Lord's Supper, which
we celebrate, in the night of Maundy Thursday be-

fore the crucifixion." Why was the thesis so cautiously formulated? Because from a certain point of view (the approach of form criticism) it is doubtful whether Jesus instituted the Lord's Supper in terms of the New Testament record. Taking this tack, a student of the New Testament must regard the cultus of the early Church as part and parcel of the composition of the texts concerned with the Lord's Supper. The event of which they speak cannot be delimited by chronologically verifiable data. But this does not mean that the Lord's Supper is no longer relevant in its present form.

Bornkamm's historical and theological rationale for the Lord's Supper is as follows. It was never instituted merely by the historical Jesus, but by Jesus Christ as Lord, which he became only through the Resurrection. Thus he inaugurated the supper, simultaneously in his person and his saving action breaking through the chronological events. The believing and worshipping Church after Easter belongs, as it were, from the beginning to the event of the institution. It is not merely an imitating and copying group of people. It witnesses to the fact that the death of Jesus, in its meaning in the light of Easter, has merged as the constituting element with the meal it celebrates.

Bornkamm does not mean to deny the probability that Jesus inaugurated the so-called Lord's Supper in some kind of meal.[44] But he wants to stress that the redemptive significance of his death entered post-factum whatever supper Jesus may have instituted. Thus historical references such as "on the night when he was betrayed" or "do this in remembrance of me" (1 Cor. 11:23–24) are of secondary importance for the understanding of the meal. The redemptive death itself is already an invitation to its proclamation and celebration.

It is a significant emphasis of Bornkamm's that the true author of the sacred meal is Jesus as risen Lord and not merely as earthly Jesus. But this also confuses the issue to a certain extent. We must distinguish three stages in the development of the Lord's Supper: (1) a meal that Jesus celebrated with his disciples before his death, which later awakened in the disciples sacred memories, since it was the last meal they had had together with their Lord; (2) the death of Jesus on the Cross; (3) the interpretation of the meaning of the Cross relative to the last meal. Bornkamm does not stress the second stage enough. As regards the third stage the community under the guidance of the Holy Spirit transformed the last meal into the Holy Supper. In spite of Jesus' death the community experienced his continuing presence. It found that God for them was ever deepening the meaning of his death. This new work of God, the ever deepening understanding of who Jesus really was, was experienced as Holy Spirit. In communion with God the community of faith was trying to understand more fully what transpired in the event of God's presence in Jesus.

Bornkamm is interested in asserting that the redemptive post-Easter history of Jesus as the Christ cannot be imprisoned in an objective history of facts. Thus he believes that the risen Lord is the real author of Holy Communion. But as important as the realization that the Church introduced a new kind of history [45] is the inquiry whether the Church adequately grasped the second stage in the development of the Lord's Supper. It is of utmost significance to learn not only that a relatively new meal is inaugurated by the risen Lord and the Church as his body, but also that the meal is an adequate representation of the significance of Jesus' death.

We have concerned ourselves with only a very small section of the field of Christian worship: the basic datum to which it refers and the first appropriation of the datum. From the very beginning Christian worship is an attempt to understand this datum. It is not the slavish execution of an arbitrary command but an interpretation, as indicated by the development of the Lord's Supper. The further history of the Lord's Supper shows the constant addition of new interpretations.[46] There is no absolute validity to any of the forms in which we today celebrate the Lord's Supper severally in our various denominations. The question may well be raised whether any single one of our forms adequately expresses the basic datum to which Christian worship refers. The lack of vigorous examination of the forms is often due to the assumption that the shape of the datum has been adequately grasped. Practically, it is inconceivable that bread and wine would ever be abandoned. Principally it is possible, however, that the Church, in a new encounter with the Holy Spirit, might proclaim the death of Jesus in a new form. What conceivably might take place is a thoroughly new interpretation of the form of Holy Communion in the light of the radically new outlook of contemporary society in philosophy, technology, and economics.[47] Primarily important is the death of Jesus and not the cultic form in which it finds expression, although this death is available to us only in some representation.

We have paid special attention to the liturgical form of the Lord's Supper. The same principal relationship at the core of this meal applies to all other cultic forms, which need as much re-examination as the sacred meal.

It should also be stressed that we have concerned ourselves only with *Christian* worship in this essay. We do well to remember that Christian worship is religiously nothing unique. Religious men, to whatever religion they belong, worship.[48] Christian worship takes its place in the transformation of man's natural worship. This process of transformation began in

Israel.[49] From the Old Testament people Christianity took over the historical orientation of the cultus. The Church, in her worship, seeks to recapture the *Heilsgeschichte*, past and present, and symbolically rehearses the meaning of her everyday activity. Christian worship, however, makes sense only if every symbolic act is permeated by an adequate understanding of the basic datum to which it refers. It is this datum that distinctly qualifies Christian worship and distinguishes it from worship in general.

We return to the beginning of our essay and Tillich's dictum that there should be no cult. As a merely ritualistic performance worship is without meaning. It also dare not be replaced by a mere ethic.[50] In man's sinful state, as long as God is not acknowledged as the ground and destiny of life by every man, Christian worship, in symbolic acts, corporately embodies the wholeness of the man who knows that the earth is the Lord's. Christian worship witnesses to man's reconciliation with God in God's participation in man's lot on the Cross. It is not cultus, paying one's respects to the deity, as much as acknowledging the true condition of man. It is a corporate manifestation of man's true being, which, of course, includes his ethical activity, but is not totally absorbed by it. Christian worship finally proclaims that all of creation shares in the redemptive act. Says Tillich: "The bread of the sacrament stands for all bread and ultimately for all nature. . . . Nature must be brought into the unity of the history of salvation. It must be delivered from its demonic bondage." [51] Christian worship in its essence affirms that this deliverance has already taken place: in the cross of Jesus God destroyed all bondage and made his world whole. It is more than cultus: it is acknowledgment of the unconcealment of the true nature of things. It is also more than an ethic: it is the ceasing of merely doing good by standing motionless in the acknowledgment of the true character of reality.

In Christian worship the true character of the Christian life is summed up. A Christian cannot organize his life in arbitrary terms. He has been claimed by the innermost character of things, the heart of creation, in God's reconciliation with his creature. In the offensive suffering on the Cross the norm of all beings is unconcealed. This does not mean that the Christian life and thus also Christian worship would have to become an exact replica of the historical datum of Calvary. God suffered in his Son that we might be *free* to use our knowledge of true being as we encounter him ever anew. Thus the Lord's Supper as well as every other act of Christian worship must partially reflect the acme of God's manifestation — his openness to all men in Jesus Christ — and partially the Christian's appropriation of this fundamental reality in a creative interpretation that draws upon the continuing self-disclosure of God in his Holy Spirit.[52]

The Christian must experience the Cross in an act of interpretation in worship. What the proper interplay of the norm and the freedom of worship might produce, who can tell? One thing seems certain, however. It calls for discarding the symbols of religious glamor in our churches. The feelings of our hearts and the thoughts of our minds are not playthings for self-enjoyment, but gifts to be offered as sacrifices of thanksgiving to God.[53]

NOTES

1. Paul Tillich, *Systematic Theology* (University of Chicago Press, 1951), I, 80.
2. Immanuel Kant, *Religion Within the Limits of Reason Alone* (Harper Torchbooks, 1960), p. 158.
3. Ibid. p. 123.
4. Hugh Anderson, "The Historical Jesus and the Origins of Christianity," *Scottish Journal of Theology*, XIII (1960), 134–5.
5. Cf. Günther Bornkamm, *Jesus of Nazareth* (Harper, 1961), pp. 188–91.
6. Joseph Sittler, *The Ecology of Faith* (Muhlenberg Press, 1961), pp. 100–101.
7. Oscar Cullmann, *Early Christian Worship* (SCM Press, 1953), p. 115.
8. Ibid.
9. Ibid. p. 48.
10. Ibid. p. 49.
11. Ibid. p. 117.
12. Ibid. p. 116.
13. Ibid. p. 58.
14. Ibid. p. 63.
15. Ibid. p. 64.
16. Ibid. p. 64.
17. Ibid. p. 66.
18. Ibid. p. 69.
19. Ibid. p. 70. Cf. also p. 118.
20. Ibid. p. 118.
21. A good case for the dependence of the Johannine tradition upon the worship of the Johannine congregations is made by Siegfried Schulz, *Untersuchungen zur Menschensohn-Christologie im Johannesevangelium* (Göttingen: Vandenhoeck und Ruprecht, 1957), p. 176.
22. The preceding paragraphs review Martin Dibelius, *Die Formgeschichte des Evangeliums* (3d ed.; Tübingen: J. C. B. Mohr, 1959), pp. 178ff.
23. Ibid. p. 189.

24. Rudolf Bultmann, *Die Geschichte der synoptischen Tradition* (4th ed.; Göttingen: Vandenhoeck und Ruprecht, 1958), p. 308.

25. Ibid. p. 287.

26. It is instructive on this score to compare a more confident view such as that of T. W. Manson in *The Servant-Messiah* (Cambridge University Press, 1953) with the more chastened approach of Bornkamm in *Jesus of Nazareth*, and both with the radically skeptical standpoint of Rudolf Bultmann in *Jesus and the Word* (Scribner's, 1934).

27. Evelyn Underhill, *Worship* (Harper, 1957), p. 111 (italics added).

28. Ibid. p. 46.

29. Ibid. p. 3.

30. Ibid. p. 4.

31. Cf., for example, ibid. p. 15: "The reality and attraction of His [God's] eternity must be experienced in time, if they are indeed to enter and transform our experience."

32. Ibid. p. 16.

33. Ibid. p. 30.

34. Ibid. p. 33.

35. Ibid. p. 37.

36. Ibid. p. 46.

37. Ibid. p. 55.

38. Ibid. p. 71 (italics added).

39. Ibid. p. 71.

40. As an example of what is possible in a local church in this respect cf. *Time*, Dec. 22, 1961, p. 42.

41. Underhill, op. cit. p. 68.

42. Peter L. Berger, *The Noise of Solemn Assemblies* (Doubleday, 1961), p. 118.

43. XXII (1962), 1–15.

44. Bornkamm, *Jesus of Nazareth*, pp. 160ff.

45. The concept of "Geschichte" with which Bornkamm operates comes very close to what traditionally has been called "Holy Spirit." The possibility of the German word "Geschichte" in a twofold sense is confusing to the point of unintelligibility when applied to the Bible.

46. Cf. Helmut T. Lehmann (ed.), *Meaning and Practice of the Lord's Supper* (Muhlenberg Press, 1961); Adolf Harnack, *History of Dogma* (Dover, 1961), II, 138ff.; Rudolf Bultmann, *The Presence of Eternity* (Harper, 1957), pp. 51ff.

47. Mergers between denominations today afford excellent opportunities for rethinking the order and the liturgical forms of the Church. The union of the Congregational Christian Churches and the Evangelical and Reformed Church in 1957 is a case in point. Douglas Horton has recently published a description of this new body: *The United Church of Christ* (Nelson, 1962). In his reflections on the sacraments, as understood in the new denomination, he cautiously yet determinedly moves in the direction we have in mind. He assures the reader: "Whatever your characteristics — whether you be a man of few words or many; of scientific or artistic frame of mind; quick thinking, deep thinking, or both — the grace of Christ in you will not go out from you in a sheer or wooden way; it will take the shape of your own interests and abilities. Christ never reduces a man to a given mold, he brings him up to his own best capacities and expressions. At the time of communion it is appropriate for each person to consider how he can best channel the grace of the Lord Jesus to his neighbor: this self-examination is part of the cost of grace" (p. 96). These thoughts are merely embryonic regarding the rethinking that might take place on the liturgical forms of the church.

Another testimony that is relevant in this context comes from the East Asia Theological Commission of the World Council of Churches. In an interim report the claim is made that "conformity of Worship to Scripture does not mean return to the precise ways of worship of the New Testament period, even if we could discover in detail what those ways were. The Church baptized and celebrated the Eucharist for many years before the first books of the New Testament were written, and their authors often assume an already established liturgical tradition. Even after the Canon of the New Testament had come to be accepted, liturgy continued to develop as part of the living tradition of the Church in some measure independently of Scripture, and yet could still claim to conform to biblical revelation." *Worship and the Church's Mission and Unity* (A Report of the Third Indian Conference on Worship held at Bangalore May 26–30, 1960. Printed at the C.L.S. Press, Bangalore-1.), 8. It is, however, not enough to say that we cannot literally accept the New Testament ways of worship as our own ways. We must understand the inner workings and the outer development of the Lord's Supper, as referred to in the New Testament, or of the Eucharist as celebrated even before the New Testament was written. The Indian report shows special interest in the so-called indigenization of worship: "Nevertheless, there is a strong desire that Indian expression of Christian worship should be cultivated and popularised. The fear of possible syncretism should not deter us from courageous ventures in this direction. As long as the centrality of Christ in the Church's worship is maintained there is no need to fear the danger of syncretism." (15) The possibility of the indigenization of worship is part of the continuing need for appropriation of the norm of worship. It is part of the responsibility of Christian freedom in worship. True progress in this area can be achieved only if the *centrality of Christ,* to which the report refers, is grasped in terms of the *shape* of the basic Christian datum.

48. A moving testimony to the universality of worship is found in Melville's *Moby Dick,* in which Ishmael worships together with his newly found bosom friend Queequeg the little idol Yojo which Queequeg is carrying around in his grip, frequently taking it out for worship. Explains Ishmael: "I was a good Christian; born and bred in the bosom of the infallible Presbyterian Church. How then could I unite with the wild idolator in worshipping his piece of wood? But what is worship? thought I. Do you suppose now, Ishmael, that the magnanimous God of heaven and earth — pagans and all included — can possibly be jealous of an insignificant bit of black wood? Impossible! But what is worship? — to do the will of God — *that* is worship. And what is the will of God? — to do to my fellow man what I would have my fellow man to do to me — *that* is the will of God. Now, Queequeg is my fellow man.

And what do I wish that this Queequeg would do to me? Why, unite with me in my particular Presbyterian form of worship. Consequently, I must then unite with him in his; ergo, I must turn idolator. So I kindled the shavings; helped prop up the innocent little idol; offered him burnt biscuit with Queequeg; salaamed before him twice or thrice; kissed his nose; and that done, we undressed and went to bed, at peace with our own conscience and all the world. But we did not go to sleep without some little chat." Herman Melville, *Moby Dick* (Grosset, 1955), pp. 67ff.

49. Cf. Hans-Joachim Kraus, *Gottesdienst in Israel* (München: Chr. Kaiser Verlag, 1954), pp. 122ff. For the transformation process in Western culture see Dom Gregory Dix, *The Shape of the Liturgy* (Dacre Press, 1944), pp. 315, 387.

50. That there is a trend even in the New Testament in this direction is clearly stated by Gerhard Delling in *Worship in the New Testament* (Westminster Press, 1962), p. 13: "A saying of James deserves attention. It is obviously a criticism of the way in which Christians pay their homage to God. In guarding against a merely external Worship it goes so far as to characterise the true expression of religion as service to the helpless and to keeping oneself unspotted from the 'world.' Obviously in the environment of the writer, taking part in Christian Worship is already largely a matter of mere form and empty appearance; that is the reason for his warning. It is clear, however, from such a theme *that Christian Worship is in danger of being entirely robbed of its meaning and its place taken by a mere ethic*" (italics added).

51. Paul Tillich, *The Protestant Era* (University of Chicago Press, 1948), pp. 111–12.

52. Cf. Delling, op. cit. pp. 23–4: "The community Worship is fundamentally the work of the Spirit. . . . Without the operation of the Spirit Christian Worship would be a merely human act. . . . Through the Spirit *Christian Worship is the act of God in the community*." Our paper has dealt with worship more from the theological point of view. Much that was left undone lies in the field of a sociological approach to worship. Possibilities for further inquiry in this area are clearly

outlined in James Gustafson, *Treasure in Earthen Vessels* (Harper, 1961), pp. 93ff.

53. A remark on the "Sitz im Leben" of this paper might help to clarify its major concern. For many of the churches in the South, worship is still a "work of art." This is certainly not a Southern problem only. But it is especially pressing in the South of 1963. Picket lines, sit-ins and boycotts have made a considerable impact on business, but little on the church. The gap between worship and life must be bridged. Imperative as the first step in liturgical reform is the desegregation of "God's lunch counter." It must be understood that "Any cultic pattern of worship, whether in the congregation or by an individual is a mummery unless the conversation and action begun before the altar is continued in every moment of man's existence." See E. S. Brown, Jr., "The Worship of the Church and the Modern Man," *Studia Liturgica*, II (1963), 60. Cf. also the words from a Communion Manual recently published by John A. T. Robinson: "The sharing of bread, concluded now sacramentally, must be continued socially—and thence economically and politically." *Liturgy Coming to Life* (London, 1960), p. 112. Robinson clearly points out why this understanding of the Lord's Supper does not countenance segregation in the church. Ibid., pp. 43, 81.

The Origin of
the Church's Liturgy

If one asks what is uniquely distinctive of Christianity in the earliest days of its common life, the answer is certainly its assurance in, and testimony to, God's fulfillment in Christ of the promises implicit and explicit in the Old Covenant. Jesus is Messiah, whose mission and triumph inaugurate the awaited age to come. Jesus is Son of God, who in his perfect obedience fulfills the Law and thus manifests the ultimate purpose of God's chosen people in history. Jesus is Servant, whose voluntary, spotless, and vicarious sacrifice brings reconciliation with God, an atonement that avails not only for Israel, but also "for many." Jesus is Son of Man, the new Adam, who in his victory over sin and death constitutes the principle of a new humanity, a new creation that has cosmic implication. Jesus is Lord, to whom everything in heaven and earth and under the earth is destined to be subject, at whose Name every creature is to bow down and obey.

Christians are living in "the last times," in that indefinable but no less real margin between Jesus' present exaltation and final epiphany, his first epiphany and ultimate exaltation. It matters little whether this end be viewed temporally as an interim between Resurrection and Second Coming, or supra-temporally as realized Presence and Judgment. The boundary between time and beyond-time, between history and eternity, between heaven and earth, is transcended. What is now made known in Christ is what God has purposed from before the foundation of the world, the fullness of time. The evident mark of this fullness is the outpouring in the end of times of the Spirit of the Lord, the Spirit of prophecy, not only upon select and chosen witnesses, but upon all who call upon the Lord's Name.

What is affirmed of Christ is applied realistically to his Church. They are made one Body, one spirit with him, joint heirs of his realm and of his glory. They also possess his anointing, and share in his fulfillment of kingship and priesthood. They, too, are sons of God by adoption and grace, and ministers of reconciliation who offer the spiritual sacrifices of a new covenant. They are a new nation, a new race that transcends the old distinction of Jew and Gentile, bond and free, male and female. And they are enthroned in heavenly places with the Lord, with whom they shall judge even the angels. This is a great mys-

tery indeed — that which concerns Christ and his
Church.

These statements, of course, compress a number
of insights that only gradually unfolded in the apostolic age and later. But they are no less implicit in
the words and actions of Jesus. He laid claim to being lord of the Sabbath, and promised his rest to all
who were weary and heavy-laden. He spoke of the
temple of his Body that would be raised up to succeed
the sanctuary on Mount Sion. Before him the law
and the prophets obtained until John; with him the
Kingdom now enters to exercise its power. At the
proper time and place and in the proper company, he
was not reticent about his Person. There is an awe-
some character to his word, at that final entry into the
holy city, when the Pharisees besought him to rebuke
the glad Hosannas of his disciples: "I tell you that,
if these should hold their peace, the stones would immediately cry out" (Luke 19:40). It is a folly of
certain critics who refuse to attribute to Jesus the
lofty and original Christology of the gospels. It is to
make meaningless all that he said and exhibited about
kingdom and covenant, lordship and judgment at the
Last Supper. There he gave the visible earnest of the
new testament that should replace the old. And this
earnest was realized in the Easter manifestation among
those who ate and drank with him after his rising from
the dead.

That which was implicit in the sayings and doings of Jesus became explicit within a generation, through the sifting of the Church in the Judaizing controversy. No set of merely historical and sociological circumstances can explain away the victory of Paul and the prominence of his letters in the New Testament. If Jewish Christianity represents a pure gospel — however much it may have modified the Old Testament by its higher criticism respecting the "false pericopes" — then there has been no trace of a pure gospel since at least the fourth century. The truth is that the facts were on Paul's side. The Holy Spirit of promise was also poured out upon and possessed by the Gentiles without reference to the Law. On this fact was broken all the binding force of cultic observance — circumcision and sabbath, fast and festival, distinctions of meat and drink. "Christ our Passover is sacrificed for us; therefore let us keep the feast" (1 Cor. 5:7–8) — proclaims not a new day nor a new festival nor a new rite, but a new age of undifferentiated worship in sincerity and truth.

I

It has long been a pastime of critics to debate whether the command of Jesus at the Last Supper, "Do this in remembrance of me," is authentic or not. More recently, thanks to the learned work of Dr. Joachim Jeremias,[1] some discussion has been devoted to the more pertinent question of what the phrase means. But one aspect of the command seems not to have received sufficient attention. Whether authentic or not, it does not say "when" or "how often" the Supper is to be repeated. This fact alone suggests that the phrase is either authentic or very primitive. It could hardly have arisen in just this form after the Sunday Eucharist became normative in the Church. One suspects that it is related to that pristine dawn of the Church's corporate life, summarized in Acts 2:46 as "continuing daily with one accord in the temple, and breaking bread from house to house." Certainly they were in the temple constantly from day to day in order to preach no less than to pray; and possibly they were also there to await the coming of the Lord. Though they were pious enough Jews, no stress is laid on their assiduous attention to sacrificial offerings or to sabbaths, new moons, and festivals.[2]

Similarly, in the evening gatherings at home, after the temple gates were shut, there is no sense of a specific cult interest unless one takes the whole undifferentiated "joy and gladness" in preaching, teaching, sharing, breaking bread, and prayers as all cult. Is it a vigil of expectancy of the Lord's return? Yet surely they must have slept sometime. How does one understand the word "fellowship" (*koinonia*)? Does it refer to the economic communism of the group, or to the worship, since the word is set down between teaching and the bread-breaking? The truth is, everything is shared, and the offering is a Eucharist and the Eucharist is an offering. Again, can one distinguish here the Eucharistic sacrament from the *Agape* meal, as so many liturgiologists try to do? Is it possible to say that one part of the meal was more sacred or more common than another? And, to the literal-minded, the Evangelist poses a mocking problem: How did so many converts meet together in such small quarters for a common meal? On the other hand, if they were scattered in numerous house-church groups, how did they maintain that unity of being "together" and of having "all things common"?

Such questions are ours, not theirs, nor even those of the evangelist. The fact is that we are dealing with people for whom time and space no longer have any significance. Though these people are still embodied and living on this earth, their real life is in the age to come. As in the seer of Patmos' vision of the heavenly Jerusalem, the holy city that is above and beyond, yet coming down, there is neither day nor night, and there is no church there and no sacrament. Yet they live continually in adoration of the Lamb and cease not day or night to sing his praise. We have no categories to define this new dimension of existence. It is too much for mortals.

There is a principle here, however, that has never been entirely lost in the later elaboration of liturgy and

worship in the Church. It is the principle Peter learned
one day in dutiful observance of the pious Jews' hours
of stated prayers: namely, no created thing is profane
and unclean. The only thing that is secular is sin. If
the Church later consecrates the first day of the week
or certain anniversaries as holy days, it is to remind
Christians that all days are holy. If it offers solemn
thanksgivings over certain material elements, it is that
all material things be sanctified thereby. Paul had the
root of the matter:

> One man esteemeth one day above another: another esteem-
> eth every day alike. Let every man be fully persuaded in his
> own mind. He that regardeth the day, regardeth it unto the
> Lord: and he that regardeth not the day, to the Lord he doth
> not regard it. He that eateth, eateth to the Lord, for he giveth
> God thanks; and he that eateth not, to the Lord he eateth not,
> and giveth God thanks. . . . For the kingdom of God is not
> meat and drink; but righteousness, and peace, and joy in the
> Holy Ghost (Rom. 14:5–6, 17).

These words, and others in Romans 14, show how Paul
understood the real difference between Judaism and
Christianity.

Primitive Christian life and worship are a daily expectation. "Give us this day our daily bread." The
morrow is at hand; indeed the morrow has already
come. No longer is there an annual Passover of remembrance and anticipation of deliverance. Only to-

day abides, with its feasting in the marriage Supper of the Lamb.

Within the apostolic age itself, unforeseen and unplanned conditions developed that necessitated certain differentiations in the Church's worship with respect to time, place, and occasion. Chief among these were the continuing delay of the end of history and the definitive break of Christianity with Judaism. Equally important was the geographical extension of the Church's mission in the Graeco-Roman world. The complete *koinonia* of the primitive Jerusalem community could not be maintained. At the least, the majority of believers had of necessity to work for a living under conditions imposed by a world order over which they had no control. The varied backgrounds, occupations, and resources of the Church's members posited problems to the Church's corporate unity. Jewish Christians might keep the sabbath; Gentile Christians were not always able to do so. A slave could not have the freedom of time enjoyed by a master. Quarters offered in hospitality to Christian worship could not accommodate the increasing size of congregations.

The stages by which the Church reordered its worship are hidden from us, even though the causes and results of it can be readily grasped. The Eucharist became a ceremonial rather than an actual meal, to accommodate larger assemblies in cramped rooms and to eliminate abuses such as Gentile converts were prone to carry over from experiences with pagan cultic banquets. Hence we have the transformation from what Dom Gregory Dix called the seven-action shape to the four-action shape of the holy Supper.[3] Initiatory rites are more carefully administered and structured to meet the necessities of heathen converts drawn to the faith without benefit of a mediate acquaintance with the ethic and promise of the Jewish Scriptures of the Old Testament. There develops a catechumenate: credal formularies for professions of faith, norms for the form, matter, and mode of baptismal washing and imparting of the Spirit.

Above all, there emerges in the apostolic age the observance of Sunday as the stated and obligatory time of worship and participation in the Eucharistic celebration. It is the continuing and continual renewal of Easter. Sunday replaces the old sabbath of Judaism, which had marked the completion and rest of the old created order. The first day of the week looks forward, not backward, as a beginning of the new age revealed in the Resurrection. It is the Lord's day, representing the ultimate Day of the Lord, the day of the Parousia. Unlike the sabbath, Sunday is not a taboo day, separate and sacrosanct from all other days; it gathers into itself, representatively as it were, the meaning of all days. It is symbol of millennium at

the end of time, when a thousand years are but as a
day that is past and as a watch in the night. Sunday
makes every week an Easter week, and is a sacrament
of time that makes present the beyond-time.

The primary structures of liturgical order that
evolved in the apostolic age are thus understandable
and acceptable, apart from any theological considera-
tions or judgments, as necessities arising from the geographical and numerical extension of Christianity,
and its decisive separation from Jewish institutions. A
further differentiation, elaboration, and crystallization
of Christian worship in the generations immediately
following the apostolic age are equally understandable
— and inevitable — in the face of new historical situations that could not have been foreseen. Basically these
new factors were twofold: one arising from within
the Church, as its membership was drawn predominantly from adherents of the religious cults and philosophies of Graeco-Roman paganism; the other arising
from without the Church through the pressures of
persecution and the virulent attacks of those who were
either ignorant or misinformed about its fundamental
tenets and practices. In the former case, the threat was
occasioned by sincere interpreters of Docetic tendencies or Gnostic systems, who would have transformed the gospel by substituting a mythological for
an historical Redeemer. In the latter case, the Church
was impelled to devise an apologetic, both defensive

and offensive, that provided a rational philosophical undergirding to its faith, ethic, and worship.

One would be naïve about the processes of history to maintain that the crisis of second-century Christianity should not have happened. But it is not always admitted that it is equally absurd to condemn the measures taken by the Catholic Church to meet this crisis. Even if we could indulge ourselves in the supposition that the Church might have foreseen and therefore forearmed itself in the event of this situation, we can hardly imagine how the Church could have forged any other instruments for the preservation and integrity of its witness than those which did emerge with the aura of apostolic tradition. One must be wary of those judgments passed upon the Catholic Church of the second century that speak of it in terms of decline or perversion of its pristine gospel, as though only those elements of Christian belief and usage are legitimate which are identifiably Hebraic. The Church valiantly continued the work of reconciliation of the Jew and the Greek, bringing together in a single truth the Word of Scripture and the Logos of philosophy.

One may well ask whether the charismata of the apostles, prophets, and teachers were not better preserved by the hierarchy of Ignatius and Polycarp than by the frenzied fanatics of the Montanists. Irenaeus is certainly a better guide to the faith of St. Paul than is

Marcion; and the very Hellenistic Clement of Alexandria has a *gnosis* nearer to the mind of St. John than
does the very Hellenistic Valentine. The liturgical order described by Justin and Hippolytus and Tertullian has a right to claim apostolic tradition, and it is
the more valuable as an independent testimony alongside the selected and edited documents that the Church
of their age collected to form the New Testament
canon.

II

Throughout the crisis of the second century the liturgy of the Church served as a conservative force,
however much it may at times have been abused by
the more extreme Gnostics. Two circumstances contributed to this, apart from the tendency observable
in all religions for forms of worship to preserve archaic
and traditional usages. One was the control of the liturgy in the hands of the hierarchy who claimed the
apostolic succession. Indeed, it is very likely that one
of the principal factors that contributed to the growth
of episcopal authority lay in the ancient presidency
of bishops as overseers of the Eucharistic meal. The
charismata needed for such managerial functions were
not of the creative and adventurous character such as
those of prophets and teachers; but they called for a
greater sense of order and efficiency. The other circumstance was the fact that the liturgy carried with it

the reading and exposition of the Scriptures — the greatest single legacy to Christian worship from Judaism. It is probable, too, that the fixation of a New Testament canon, in direct response to Marcion's experiment, was intended to provide Catholic Christian worship with an apostolic norm whereby the reading and interpretation of the Old Testament at the assemblies of worship might be controlled.

The forms of Christian prayer and praise were likewise derived from Judaism, more particularly as these forms had passed through the somewhat Hellenized reshaping of the Greek-speaking synagogues of the Dispersion. The oldest and best examples are the prayers of the Didache and the First Epistle of Clement, and the psalms and hymns provided in the prologue of Luke's Gospel, the Book of Revelation, and the Odes of Solomon. The structure of these forms originates in the Jewish "Benedictions," which consist of ascriptions of praise to God in his manifold attributes of creating and redeeming activity, with *anamneses* or recitals of his memorable works, and doxologies of acclamation. The language is predominantly biblical, though in the Greek dress of these formularies there appear certain terms drawn from current philosophy, whether Stoic or Platonic. Certain types include petitions in place of the recitals of the *memorabilia* of God, but these petitions are pleas for the continuing activity of God's gracious will for his people, in forgiveness, protection and deliverance, and in the final fulfillment of his purpose in the gathering of his elect into his kingdom.[4] Eduard Norden has analyzed the formal stylistic features of these prayers and hymns, and has shown that they are an "Oriental" type, different from the classic Greek forms by reason of a preference for the relative clause or the predicate participle to describe the attributes of God, and their constant use of "parallelism" of phrases so characteristic of the structure of Semitic poetry.[5] The use of the relative clause and of the predicate rather than the substantive participle is especially significant, for it reveals a conception of God in terms of his activity rather than of his essential being. Christian prayer is also proclamation of the mighty works of God, set within a framework of praise and thanksgiving.

The great liturgies of later times never lost this basic style and form, however much they were rhetorically elaborated.[6] One has only to read through the formularies of such liturgies as those of St. Basil, St. Chrysostom, St. James, or the solemn prefaces of the Latin rites to recognize at once the recital-celebration of what God has revealed and done. Justin Martyr is witness to the early formulation of this liturgical type; and the oldest, complete liturgy that is extant, that contained in the *Apostolic Tradition* of Hippolytus, is in the form of a Jewish "giving of thanks" with a recital of the *kerugma* of redemption in Christ inter-

woven with biblical and philosophical phrases. It concludes with a petition for the sending of the Holy
Spirit and a doxology.

The Eucharistic consecration prayer in Hippolytus,
as also in the later liturgies, clearly exhibits a direct
descent from the Jewish benedictions, or giving of
thanks, recited at meals, whether of a cultic or non-
cultic character. Not only the form, but the basic content of the prayer are simply Christian translations of
the three fundamental themes of these Jewish table
blessings: the creation and provident activity of God,
the redemption of his people and formation of the
covenant-community, and the fulfillment of his promise for the final establishment of his kingdom. The
theme of creation and providence was maintained in
the Christian formularies as a direct affirmation of the
beauty, goodness, and beneficent order of the world
that God had made, in conscious opposition to the
Gnostic heresy. The redemption theme obviously celebrated the work of Christ instead of the Jewish recalling of the deliverance from Egypt. And the specific recounting of the institution at the Last Supper
provided the Christian statement of the inauguration
of the new covenant. The petition for the descent of
the Holy Spirit marked the peculiarly Christian viewpoint regarding the "last times," since the gift and
presence of the Spirit were the manifest sign of the
dawn of the eschatological event, the earnest of promised age to come.

In the early centuries the celebrants were not bound to a fixed form of words to express these themes. Hence one may understand the variations of theological emphasis and perspective. Hippolytus' prayer, for example, shows his peculiar way of expressing his Christological doctrine: Christ is "Logos inseparable" from the Father prior to the Incarnation; he is "manifested Son" in the Incarnation. These variables are, if one may say so, accidental. They in no way affect the primary tradition by which celebrants were expected to "offer thanks" over the bread and the wine. The three basic themes were fixed, however much an individual officiant might enlarge upon one or another of them according to his inspiration. Later, when definition of essential doctrine became more precise, the older freedom of celebrants was restricted by officially authorized formularies, in order to ensure for the people the orthodoxy of these liturgical recitals. Variation in the forms was maintained, however, in the Eastern Churches by the use of several optional *anaphorae;* in the Western Churches by a rich adaptation of the prayers to the manifold changes of theme in the annual cycle of the Christian Year.

III

Of the utmost significance was the emergence in the second century of the Christian pattern of observance of the Pascha. This is not to say that the Church had not celebrated the Pascha from the very beginning of its historic life. There are traces of it in the letters of Paul, the Gospel of Mark, and the Book of Acts. The controversy over Quartodecimanism in the second century reveals also a tradition that reached back into apostolic times.

On the face of it, the Quartodeciman controversy might seem an irrelevant fuss over legalistic minutiae of days, months, and seasons. But there was a profound principle involved: namely, whether the Church's worship should be bound to the enactments of the old Jewish Law. The opponents of Quartodeciman practice were certainly correct in viewing it as a relic of Judaizing, of an observance according "to the letter" and not "understood by faith" according to the spirit. The Christian Pascha had a twofold dimension. For the Church living in time and history, it was a commemoration of a past event of salvation and deliverance comparable to the Jewish recalling of the Exodus at Passover. But the Church also lived in heaven, whither the Lord was exalted; and the Pascha was more than a commemoration of history. It was also participation in the eschatological triumph of the Lord and the times of renewal of the world to come.

The decision of the majority of the Churches, later ratified ecumenically at Nicaea, always to observe the Pascha on the Sunday following the spring full moon, satisfied all the conditions needful for a meaningful observance. Its dating was still related to the Passover, to the salvation event of the old covenant that was the type of the salvation event of the new. It still depended upon that conjunction in the order of nature of vernal equinox and full moon that tied it to specific time in the order of temporal existence. But by placing it always on a Sunday it expressed without reference to a legal, Jewish holy day, the new quality of life typified by the day of the Resurrection. Furthermore, it made possible a harmony of the variant chronologies of the Gospels with regard to the date of the Lord's Passion. For all four Gospels agreed on the one datum: namely, the Lord had suffered on a Friday and been raised on a Sunday.

The pattern of the Paschal observances, by the latter part of the second century at the latest, was basically uniform in all the churches, with only minor variations in detail. It consisted of a strict fast on the Friday and Saturday — the days "when the Bridegroom was taken away" — during which the candidates for Baptism were given a final testing and screening. A vigil followed on Saturday evening; and in the middle of the night the initiatory ceremonies of Baptism and Confirmation were administered. When these were completed, the festal Eucharist of Easter Day was celebrated without delay at the pre-dawn hour of the Resurrection of the Lord. The entire complex of ceremony and observance was considered as a reliving, sacramentally, of the redemptive exodus of the Lord.

In him and through him the Church passed over from death to life, from sin to righteousness, from bondage to freedom, from life under law to life in the Spirit.

Though viewed as a single whole, the Paschal experience was at the same time differentiated into both a once-for-all and an ever-repeated act, conformable to the two planes of existence in which the Church lived. As Christ died and rose again once, in a never-to-be-repeated event of history, which at the same time was the summation of the meaning of history for all eternity, so the Christian was initiated into his death and resurrection once, in a never-to-be-repeated sacramental act that was the earnest of his eternal inheritance and his deliverance from the powers of the present age of sin and death. By Baptism and Confirmation the Christian was made alive unto God for ever and a partaker of the Holy Spirit of promise. Nonetheless he was still bound, until released by physical death, to the suffering and tribulation of the present time, and was therefore in need of the continual nourishment of spiritual food and drink to strengthen him against the trials and corrupting elements of the world. Hence the Eucharistic banquet of the Paschal rite was repeated Sunday after Sunday so long as he lived in this age, on the day that recalled and renewed the primary Easter experience, giving the Christian foretaste in the here and now of the unending joy and feasting in the marriage Supper of the Lamb. It is in this sense, surely, that one must understand the bold Ignatian phrase about the "breaking of bread, which is the medicine of immortality, the antidote that we should not die but live for ever in Jesus Christ." [7]

Participation in the Paschal observance and the Sunday Eucharist was an obligation upon every Christian — not by reason of any law, though it was to become such by later canonical legislation. The obligation was inherent in the Christian's understanding of who he was and to whom he belonged. The fact that Christians willingly risked their lives every week to do together this Eucharist, this Paschal sacrament, is sufficient testimony both to its voluntary as well as to its obligatory character. And it says a great deal for the intelligence of the Roman magistracy that it persecuted Christians not because of their supposedly superstitious belief that Jesus was a god, but because of their obstinacy in assembling themselves together to read the Scriptures and do the Eucharist. It is only the modern heresy of indifference that allows many Christians today to think that religion is "what the individual does with his own solitariness," [8] or that attendance upon the Word and Sacrament on Sundays is a matter of option provided only that he be a sincere believer and a kindly neighbor. The Romans did not put the aged Polycarp to the stake for such lovable virtues.

It is interesting that Tertullian, after his adherence

to the Spirit-directed sect of the Montanists, should have upbraided the Catholics because they did not impose the obligation of other fasts than the one preceding the Pascha. The fact is that many devout Catholics of his time observed additional ascetic exercises, though always on a voluntary basis. And these exercises were themselves only extensions of the Paschal celebration. Thus one should understand the development of the "station" days of fasting and prayer, and in some places of additional participation in the Eucharist: namely, Wednesdays and Fridays. For these days made each week a renewal of Holy Week, commemorating the betrayal and crucifixion that preceded the Sunday commemoration of the Resurrection. Similarly, in his exposition of the daily hours of prayer — what later developed into the canonical hours of monastic observance — Hippolytus signified each time of devotion in the twenty-four hour round from cockcrow to cockcrow as a following of the Passion and Resurrection, especially as its sequence is laid out in the Gospel of Mark. His scheme was as profound as it was ingenious.[9]

The sequence begins at cockcrow with the memory of the denial of the Christ by the Jewish Sanhedrin — and, had Hippolytus not been such a good Roman Christian, he might have added the denial of Peter also. At Terce, the Lord was condemned by Pilate; at Sext, he was crucified. At Nones, he descended into hell; at Vespers, his mortal body was laid in the tomb. Midnight marks the pause of all creation as it awaits his coming. The Resurrection (and shall we say also the Parousia?) completes the cycle at the new cock-crow before the dawn. In actual time the commemoration is but a day. Yet Hippolytus finds here not one day, but the three days' span of Paschal renewal from Good Friday to Easter, by counting the three hours darkness from noon to Nones as a night between two days. Possibly this way of reckoning was more congenial to the Mediterranean mind, accustomed as it was to the afternoon siesta. But the pattern of the canonical hours can seem artificial only to the man who cannot appreciate a devotion that makes every day and night a reliving with Christ of death and resurrection.

The second-century Church made one other contribution to the liturgy of Paschal renewal: namely, the Eucharistic celebration of the anniversaries of the martyrs. There is something too profound for words in this Christian transformation of the Gentiles' cult of the departed. Only the Pascha and what the Pascha signified could have produced the celebration of a death day as a "birthday." The martyr's triumph was Christ's triumph. His victory was the consummation in eternity of what had been already accomplished for him in time — both historically in the once-for-all salvation event of Cross and empty tomb, and sacramentally in the once-for-all Paschal initiation into the death and resurrection of the Lord. The Eucharistic banquet on the day of the martyr was the Church's completion of the feast that began in the vigil of the martyr's trial and the baptism of his blood.

I V

The triumph of Christianity over its competitors for the allegiance of the ancient world, which followed upon the conversion of Constantine, brought in its train two significant enrichments to its liturgical inheritance. Both were responsive to the new situation in which the Church found itself vis-à-vis the state and society of the world, in order that it might bring them into subjection to Christ and permeate and transform them with the values and aims of the City of God.

On the one hand, there was the adoption of a second festival focus in the annual round of the year — the celebration of the Birthday of the Son of God, the appearance in the world of the Word made flesh. It was the final transformation and consecration by the Church of the *praeparatio evangelica* among the Gentiles. It was the Christian fulfillment of the long yearning of the heathen for concrete identification with a saviour-god expressed in hero-cult and ruler-worship. And at the same time it was the Christian fulfillment of philosophy's quest for a monotheistic devotion and a

cosmic redeemer. It is significant that the Church selected for this festival the winter solstice, the im-
movable center of the solar year that marked the renewing of the fixed round of the universe in a stable
and rational order that was itself an earnest of hope
for the dawn of a new age. Thus the Incarnation festival of the Birthday of the "Sun of Rightousness" replaced the last movement toward monotheistic faith
in the pagan world in its celebration of the birthday of
the Unconquered Sun. (Perhaps in this adoption of
Christmas, Constantine himself — converted from sun-
worship to Christ — had a hand.) Conjointly, the link-
ing of Epiphany and Christmas brought into the em-
brace of the Incarnation festival the more ancient
mythological syncretism of the East which had developed at Alexandria (the meeting place of Greek and
Oriental in the pre-Christian era) — the birthday of
the new Aeon (age) from the virgin mother Kore.
And this Epiphany festival, too, marked a more ancient winter solstice in the East.

Yet the Church's Incarnation festival at the turn
of the solar year was no more mythological than its
Resurrection festival at the spring moon of the lunar
year. It marked the commemoration of an actual historical birth, of the child Jesus born in Bethlehem of
Judaea of the Virgin Mary his mother, a birth marked
by a super-cosmic sign in the heavens that brought
to worship at his crib the Magi of the Gentiles. Thus

with the "star" that "stood over where the young child was," we may comprehend the manifestation of the Logos by whom all worlds were made, the only-begotten of the Father and Creator of heaven and earth, in the concrete, historical humanity of Jesus the Christ. So is consummated the real and essential union of the divine and the human, the universal and the particular, the mythological and the historical.

Nor is this all. The development of the Incarnation festival was contemporaneous with the struggle of the Church in the fourth and fifth centuries to define its monotheistic-trinitarian faith and its Christological doctrine. The great ecumenical Creeds of Nicaea and Chalcedon are the bulwarks that prevent the Incarnation festivals from degenerating either into a mythological mystery rite (like the birth of Aeon from Kore) or a secular birthday celebration of a god-made-manifest in the temporal ruler of a totalitarian state that has deified itself. Henceforth, both the cosmic Sun and the Roman emperor cease to be gods and give place to that "one and the same Son, our Lord Jesus Christ" who is "of one substance with the Father as regards his Godhead, and at the same time of one substance with us as regards his manhood." So the Creed of Chalcedon.

Nor should we overlook the significant fact that the Church has never celebrated the birthday of any other historical person, except for the two representative precursors of its incarnate Lord: the prophet John the Baptist and the Lord's virgin mother Mary. In this reticence of the Church to include birthdays in its liturgical commemorations, we understand the fundamental and original orientation of its observance of times and seasons. For the true birthday of each and every one of its members is the experience of death and resurrection in the water and the blood. It is not our birthday in time that is significant in the household of faith, but our birthday in eternity.

As with Easter and Pentecost, so with Christmas and Epiphany, the liturgy involves more than mere historical commemoration. The Incarnation festivals look forward no less than backward. It is not that Christmas is chronologically prior to Good Friday and Easter. Of course, the Son who must suffer and die and rise again must first be born. He must become man in order that in and through our humanity he might redeem man. But more than this, the Church surrounds the Incarnation festival in an eschatological frame, making the seasons that precede and follow Christmas and Epiphany a time of Advent expectation of the Second Coming of the Lord — not in humility but in glory. As the Church of the old covenant awaited his coming in historic fulfillment of the divine promise, so the Church of the new covenant awaits his coming in supra-historical fulfillment of the divine promise — no longer in the spotless garment of sinless flesh, but in the glorious apparel of his final epiphany when he shall deliver up the Kingdom to God and His Father. The gospel of Christmas and Epiphany is the same gospel as that of Easter and Pentecost: "the Word was made flesh . . . and we beheld his glory"; "this same Jesus, which is taken up from you into heaven, shall so come in like manner as ye have seen him go into heaven."

The second important development of the Church's liturgy after the peace under Constantine was the creation of the Divine Office by the monastic communities out of the older tradition of daily hours of prayer observed in private devotion. By day and by night, this corporate prayer of representative communities of the Church's clergy and laity unites with the ceaseless worship of heaven in lifting up the world no less than the Church in the praise and supplication of God. The Divine Office is the sanctification of all of time and the instrument by which all creation is continually responsive to its Creator.

The ascetic vocation to this lifelong office of prayer is one of the Spirit's charismatic gifts to the Church, as necessary to its edification as the gifts of prophecy, teaching, or healing. To deny this is to deny the efficacy of disinterested worship. It is the reaching out of the Church to its otherworldliness, framed as it is within the most disciplined ordering of time and regulated communal life and labor. In the ideal toward which it strives, the vocation of those communities whose chief purpose is the recital of the Divine Office is model and pattern of that *koinonia*, that sharing of all things in common, which is the leaven of the Kingdom of God in the lump of an earthly, sinful Church.

It is not surprising, therefore, that the heart of the Divine Office — the very essence of it — is the continual recital of the Psalter. Through the Psalter, the Church makes its own the prayer-book of its Lord. It prays the Psalms as he prayed them, commemorating in them the Psalms' prophetic witness to Christ, and realizing through them his selfsame trust and resignation, obedience, and hope. For the Psalms are the representative worship of the Israel of God as the purpose and destiny of that Israel is completed in the prayer and praise of the beloved Son. The particular historic or cultic situations for which the several Psalms were composed are largely lost to us. That they have such roots in the particularities of history is evident. But they have been made a universal, communal voice — first in their adaptation for the worship of the older people of God, then extended by the Church, through its "Christologizing" [10] of them, to be the thankful and suppliant offering of all those who are now or shall be numbered among the redeemed. So the Psalms carry on the continual antiphon between heaven and earth, between the cry of anguish, "How

long shall mine enemy triumph over me?" and the as-
suring response, "O give thanks unto the Lord, for
he is gracious; because his mercy endureth for ever."

V

Since the sixth century there has been no major creative development of the liturgy. The history of the
Church's liturgical worship has been one of successive
and variant periods of elaboration, revision, deforma-
tion, and recovery. Our present age bids fair to become one of the times of recovery. At least the ecumenical encounter has brought into sharper focus the
comprehensive picture of the fullness of the Church's
liturgical tradition and made possible a more impar-
tial appreciation and evaluation of it.

The liturgy is essentially the means and instrument
of both the proclamation and the appropriation by
the Church of its redeeming Lord and his redemptive
acts. By prophetic word and sacramental deed, the
Church witnesses to itself and to the world the salvation of God, and at the same time actualizes within its
own corporate body a real earnest of that salvation.
It experiences and knows through the instrumentality
of the liturgy both what it is and what it shall become.
It comprehends in the here and now both what it has
been made by grace and what it shall be in glory.
Though its redemption has been accomplished once-
for-all, it is continually renewed and increased by
the Holy Spirit of promise, until the consummation

of all things at the end of time and unto the ages of ages. So its liturgy orders its life in time that it may lay hold upon the eternal realities.

To date, the history of Christianity has been in the main a "Western" history. The liturgical "canon" (if we may so speak) of this "Western" Christianity has been fourfold: Baptism and Eucharist, Christian Year and Divine Office. It need not be a closed "canon." It is a "canon" that the Church has evolved, by providential inspiration, in uniting into one the Jew and the Greek. It is a "canon" that has been accepted without major alteration by the Roman, the Celt, the Teuton, and the Slav. For these peoples in their acceptance of the Christian gospel have accepted with that gospel a culture superior to their own.

Today, however, the gospel is penetrating into many cultures as ancient, as rich, and as mature, as that of the Near East in the time Christianity was born in the "fullness of time." What creative contribution and addition to the Western liturgical "canon" these ancient cultures and philosophies, especially those of the Far East, will make, no one can tell. Whether the liturgical tradition of western Christianity will be preserved, and — more than that — become a creative factor in a wider and more comprehensive synthesis, this too we do not know. But it may be affirmed without doubt that the survival of the Western liturgical tradition is dependent upon whatever recovery of its fullness the ecumenical endeavor of our generation achieves.

NOTES

1. *Die Abendmahlsworte Jesu* (3rd ed. rev.; Göttingen: Vanden-hoeck und Ruprecht, 1959; English translation of the second edition by Arnold Ehrhardt: *The Eucharistic Words of Jesus*, Macmillan, 1955).

2. For the discussion of this and the following paragraphs, and for much of section III, one may refer to my more extended treatment and documentation in *The Paschal Liturgy and the Apocalypse* (Ecumenical Studies in Worship, No. 6; Lutter-worth Press — John Knox Press, 1960).

3. This is the principal thesis of his famous work, *The Shape of the Liturgy* (Dacre Press, 1944).

4. Cf. J. P. Audet, "Literary Forms and Content of a Normal Εὐχαριστία in the First Century," *Studia Evangelica* (Texte und Untersuchungen, 73; Berlin: Akademie Verlag, 1959), pp. 643–62.

5. *Agnostos Theos, Untersuchungen zur Formengeschichte re-ligiöser Rede* (Leipzig-Berlin: B. G. Teubner, 1913), pp. 143ff.

6. See my paper, "The Formation and Influence of the Antiochene Liturgy," *Dumbarton Oaks Papers* xv (Washington, 1961), pp. 25–44.

7. Ignatius of Antioch, *Ephesians* 20:2.

8. The phrase is that of Professor Alfred North Whitehead, *Religion in the Making* (Lowell Lectures, 1926; Macmillan, 1927), p. 16, though, of course, he employs it in another context.

9. Hippolytus, *Apostolic Tradition* (ed. G. Dix; S.P.C.K., 1937), xxxvi (pp. 62ff.).

10. Cf. Balthasar Fischer, *Die Psalmenfrömmigkeit der Märtyrer-kirche* (Freiburg: Herder, 1949), p. 6.

ALEXANDER SCHMEMANN

Theology and Liturgical Tradition

The problem of the relationship between worship and theology is on the theological agenda of our time. Several factors, moreover, seem to indicate that it is an urgent problem — the victorious growth of liturgical movements in practically all Christian denominations, the ecumenical encounter,* the rediscovery of symbolism as an essential religious category, and, finally, the theological revival with its radical *examen de conscience* concerning the very nature of theological inquiry. The *leitourgia* of the Church has become for the theologian a challenge that has to be evaluated and answered in theological terms. And even those who denounce this growing interest in worship as dangerous (e.g. Karl Barth) must do so on theologi-

* According to Professor Joseph Sittler, it acknowledges "the fact that the way Christian people worship is declarative of what they believe. This declaration as made in worship may well be of a depth and fullness seldom attained in credal propositions."

165

cal grounds, within a consistent theology of worship.

Although the existence of the problem is certain, it is still difficult to define it. There is much confusion and ambiguity in the use of certain terms. One speaks, for example, of liturgical theology, of a liturgical "resourcement" of theology. For some, this implies an almost radical rethinking of the very concept of theology, a complete change in its structure. The *leitourgia* — being the unique expression of the Church, of its faith and of its life — must become the basic *source* of theological thinking, a kind of *locus theologicus* par excellence. There are those, on the other hand, who, while admitting the importance of the liturgical experience for theology, would rather consider it as a necessary *object* of theology — an object requiring, first of all, a theological clarification of its nature and function. Liturgical theology or the theology of liturgy — we have here two entirely different views concerning the relationship between worship and theology. And this difference implies much more than a difference of emphasis. Our attempt here is designed to clarify, very briefly and, so to say, tentatively, at least a few of these implications.

I

To understand the real nature of the two tendencies mentioned here, we must remember that both have antecedents in the past, and are based to some extent on a conscientious desire to recover positions that are supposed to have been held previously. And, indeed, one can discern in the history of the Church two main types or patterns of relationship between theology and the *leitourgia:*

(1) *The patristic type.* The recent revival of patristic studies shows that one of the major characteristics of the Fathers is precisely that of an organic connection between their theological thought and their liturgical experience. *Lex orandi est lex credendi:* this axiom means that the liturgical tradition, the liturgical life, is a natural milieu for theology, its self-evident term of reference. The Fathers do not "reflect" on liturgy. For them it is not an *object* of theological inquiry and definition, but rather the living source and the ultimate criterion of all Christian thought: "Our opinion is in accordance with the Eucharist, and the Eucharist in turn establishes our opinion," said St. Irenaeus.* We shall have to deal with this position later on. At this point let us simply state that it existed, and that there is nothing fortuitous in the claim sometimes put forward by the liturgical movement that it constitutes a return to this patristic ideal.

(2) *The scholastic type.* By "scholastic" we mean, in this instance, not a definite school or period in the

---

* *Adv. haer.* iv. 18, 5: Nostra autem consonans est sententia Eucharistiae, et Eucharistia rursus confirmat sententiam nostram (ed. Harvey ii, 205).

history of theology, but a theological structure which existed in various forms in both the West and the East, and in which all "organic" connection with worship is severed. Theology here has an independent, rational status; it is a search for a system of consistent categories and concepts: *intellectus fidei*. The position of worship in relation to theology is reversed: from a *source* it becomes an *object*, which has to be defined and evaluated within the accepted categories (e.g. definitions of sacraments). Liturgy supplies theology with "data," but the method of dealing with these data is independent of any liturgical context. Moreover, the selection and classification of the data themselves are already a "product" of the accepted conceptual structure.

From the point of view which interests us here, it is of paramount importance that, in spite of all the developments and variations of Christian theology, it is this second type that has had a monopoly from the end of the patristic age up to our own time. A good example is the Eastern Orthodox Church, justly considered to be the liturgical Church par excellence. The student of Orthodox theology knows that in all its post-patristic developments — late Byzantine theology (with the possible exception of the "hesychast" movement), the school of Kiev in the sixteenth-seventeenth centuries, Russian "academic" theology, contemporary Greece, etc. — liturgical tradition has played practically no role, and has been almost totally ignored, even as a *locus theologicus*. Liturgy and theology have peacefully co-existed — the former in its traditional form, the latter as a sacred science — with no attempt made to correlate their respective languages.

In the West the situation was somewhat different. Instead of a peaceful co-existence, there was a direct impact of theological speculation (medieval, post-tridentine) on the very forms of liturgical life. The changes were so substantial that, according to some Roman Catholic leaders of the liturgical movement, nothing short of a real liturgical reformation can restore the true liturgical tradition. The Reformers protested against the medieval theology of worship, but in spite of their desire for a return to the primitive tradition, they actually replaced this medieval doctrine by another theology of worship, so that in the Protestant Churches the *leitourgia* remained a function of its theological conception and interpretation. Subsequent developments in Roman Catholic and Protestant theology did not alter this situation. Intellectual or anti-intellectual, liberal or pietistic, theology not only remained internally independent of worship, but claimed the right to control it, and to form it according to the *lex credendi*.

The liturgical movement is the first attempt to break this monopoly, to restore to liturgical tradition its own theological status. In this it radically differs from all ritualistic or pietistic revivals of the past, with their emphasis on the psychology or the edifyingly mystical atmosphere of worship — on the "mood setting devices made available by the application of psychological categories," to quote Professor Sittler. Its fundamental presupposition is that the liturgy not only has a theological meaning and is declarative of faith, but that it is the living norm of theology; it is in the liturgy that the sources of faith — the Bible and tradition — become a living reality. The leaders and participants of the liturgical movement advocate a return to what they consider to be the essence of the patristic age, and in the name of this return denounce the other, the scholastic type, as a deviation from the genuine Christian norm of theology.

I I

It is at this point that the question must be asked: Can either of these two attitudes, in their pure expression, be acceptable to us today, and be the starting point of a reconsideration of the relationship between worship and theology? It seems to me that in the modern discussion of the liturgical problem, one essential fact is very often overlooked, or at least not given sufficient attention. Yet it is this fact that makes the liturgical problem of our time much more complex than it may seem. I define it as the *metamorphosis of the liturgical conscience.*

When we speak of the "liturgical tradition" of the early Church (the one implied in patristic theology) we must keep in mind that this tradition was constituted by two basic elements, equally essential for its proper understanding: (a) a formal continuity of Christian *leitourgia* with the Jewish worship, which supplied the Church with the basic liturgical structures (the "ordo" or "typos," the liturgical language); and (b) the radical transformation of the spirit of worship — i.e. of the meaning attached to these structures and forms. Both elements have been studied and stressed in many recent works on the history of Christian worship, but it seems to me that not all the necessary conclusions have been drawn. Yet it is only when these two fundamental categories are seen in their relationship to each other that one can understand the real nature of the patristic use of liturgy, and also of the *metamorphosis* which marked the post-patristic liturgical developments.

We know today that the cult of the early Church was essentially a Jewish cult, that practically all its forms can be traced back to Jewish antecedents, including the sacramental worship which was for a long time ascribed to the non-Jewish "mystery cults" of the Graeco-Roman world. Every year some new study widens and strengthens our knowledge of the Jewish background and the Jewish connotations of early Christian liturgy. But the liturgiologists and the historians to whom we are indebted for these studies are not always aware that this formal continuity implied a radical transformation in terms of a new *content* put in the old forms, of a Christian cult growing from Judaic roots. The Jewish *Kiddusha* gives its pattern to the Christian Eucharist, the Jewish baptism — whatever it was — to the Christian baptism. But the transformation remains within "cultual" categories; it is a transformation of the cult. In fact, this transformation took place at a much deeper level, and this seems to me the essential fact in the formation of the Christian liturgical tradition.

Paradoxically, to make a long story short, one can say that this transformation consists in *the abolishment of cult as such*, or at least in the complete destruction of the old philosophy of cult. The Christian *leitourgia* is not a "cult" if by this term we mean a sacred action, or rite, performed in order to establish "contact" between the community and God, whatever the meaning and the nature of such contact. A "cult" by its very essence presupposes a radical distinction between the "sacred" and the "profane," and, being a means of reaching or expressing the "sacred," it posits all the non-sacred as "profane." The Jewish worship was a cult in the deepest meaning of this term. In spite of all its uniqueness, of all its opposition to pagan cults, it shared with the latter this basic distinction between the "sacred" and the "profane," this function of being a means of communication between the "sacred" and the "profane." It was based on a priestly order, and on the principle of a complete isolation of the cultual action from the "profane" areas of life.

From this point of view the Christian *leitourgia* did not originate as a cult. It was not a cult, because within the *ecclesia* — the royal priesthood, the holy people, the peculiar nation — the distinction between the sacred and the profane, which is the very condition of cult, has been abolished. The Church is not a natural community which is "sanctified" through the cult. In its essence the Church is the presence, the actualization in this world of the "world to come," in this *aeon* — of the Kingdom. And the mode of this presence, of this actualization of the new life, the new *aeon*, is precisely the *leitourgia*. It is only within this eschatological dimension of the Church that one can understand the nature of the liturgy: to actualize and realize the identity of the *ecclesia* with the new *aeon*, of the "age to come."

Thou didst not cease to do all things until thou hadst brought us back to heaven, and hadst endowed us with thy kingdom which is to come. (Anaphora of St. John Chrysostom.)

The *leitourgia*, therefore, is not a cultual action performed in the Church, on its behalf, and for it; it is the action of the Church itself, or the Church *in actu*, it is the very expression of its life. It is not opposed to the non-cultual forms or aspects of the *ecclesia*, because the *ecclesia* exists in and through the *leitourgia*, and its whole life *is a leitourgia*. This life is rooted in the sacraments of Baptism and Eucharist, and the sacraments according to the early Christian understanding are precisely the means of the eschatological life of the Church. They manifest the "coming aeon" in this world, and they are themselves but the expressions of the Church as the visible sign of the Kingdom which is to come, its anticipation in time and history.

If the *leitourgia* has not only preserved the form of a cult, but can be described as a real continuation of the Jewish cult, it is to be explained in terms of the same Christian eschatology. The latter has been expressed in the antinomical formula: "*in* the world, but not *of* the world." The Church belongs to the age to come, but dwells in "this world," and its proper mission is to witness to the *eschaton* — the Lordship of Christ until He comes, until the consummation of time. In this world, the *eschaton* — the holy, the sacred, the "otherness" — can be expressed and manifested only as "cult." Not only in relation to the world, but in relation to itself as dwelling in the world, the Church must use the forms and language of the cult, in order eternally to transcend the cult, to "become what it is." And it is this "transition" of the cult — the cult which itself fulfills the *reality* to which it can only point, which it can announce, but which is the consummation of its function as cult — that we call sacrament.

Thus the liturgical tradition of the Church is fundamentally antinomical in its nature. It is a cult which eternally transcends itself, because it is the cult of a community which eternally realizes itself, as the Body of Christ, as the Church of the Holy Spirit, as ultimately, the new *aeon* of the Kingdom. It is a tradition of forms and structures, but these forms and structures are no longer those of a "cult," but those of the Church itself, of its life "in Christ." Now we can understand the real meaning of the patristic use of liturgical tradition. The formula *lex orandi est lex credendi* means nothing else than that theology is *possible* only within the Church, i.e. as a fruit of this new life in Christ, granted in the sacramental *leitourgia*, as a witness to the eschatological fullness of the Church, as, in other terms, a participation in this *leitourgia*. The problem of the relationship between liturgy and theology is not for the Fathers a problem of priority or authority. Liturgical tradition is not an "authority" or a *locus theologicus;* it is the ontological condition of theology, of the proper understanding of *kerygma*, of the Word of God, because it is in the Church, of which the *leitourgia* is the expression and the life, that the sources of theology are functioning as precisely "sources."

III

For reasons that have been partially explained and partially are still to be explained, this understanding of
the liturgical tradition has not been preserved within
the Church, and it is here that we approach the *metamorphosis* of the liturgical conscience, mentioned
above. It is not Christian worship that changed, but
it is comprehension by the believers, by the Christian
community. In a simplified form one can say that, in
the conscience of the community, the *leitourgia* became once again a cult, i.e. a system of sacred actions
and rites, performed in the Church, for the Church
and by the Church, yet in order not to make the
Church "what it is," but to "sanctify" individual
members of the Church, to bring them in contact with
God. The categories of the sacred and the profane
came back, and became categories within the Church
itself. One can study this transformation from many
points of view — the doctrine of ministry, the forms
of Church government, the relations between clergy
and laity, etc. — but here we shall limit ourselves to
the liturgical sphere proper.

The Byzantine period in the history of the Eastern
Orthodox worship is a very good example. It was
marked by the progressive "sacralization" of the
clergy, the appearance of the iconostasis separating
the sanctuary from the congregation, and finally the

transformation of the *laicos*, the member of the Body of Christ and the citizen of the Kingdom, into the *cosmikos*, or the "layman" in the actual acceptance of this term. The liturgy became a separate activity, a "means of grace" sharply opposed to all other spheres of Church life — condemned to a progressive "profanization."

This *metamorphosis* deeply marked theological thinking. One example is sufficient. In the study of the Eucharist, theological attention was focused exclusively upon the question: what happens to the elements, and how and when exactly does it happen? For the early Church the real question was: what happens to the *Church* in the Eucharist? The difference is radical; it shows perfectly clearly the nature of the change, from the eschatological to the ecclesiological "dimension" of the sacraments. Theology shifted to a purely "cultual" inquiry, which is centered always on the question of the validity and modality of a rite. Considering the sacrament exclusively from the point of view of the elements (transubstantiation, consubstantiation, etc.), theology practically ignored the liturgy itself, considering it as a non-essential, symbolical "framework" for the minimum of action and words necessary for validity. The whole liturgical action ceased to be understood as *sacramental*, i.e. as a series of transformations ultimately leading the Church, the *ecclesia*, into the fullness of the Kingdom, the only real "condition" of the transformation of the elements. This *metamorphosis* of the liturgical conscience makes it impossible to accept the choice between "liturgical theology" and a "theology of the liturgy" as valid. For the liturgy has to be explained once again as the *leitourgia of the Church* — and this is the task of the theologian. But for this task, the real liturgical tradition must be rediscovered — and this is the task of the liturgiologist. If it is for theology to purify the liturgy, it is for the liturgy to give back to theology that eschatological fullness, which the liturgy alone can "actualize" — the participation in the life of the Kingdom which is still to come.

> According to the measure of our possibilities,
> O Christ, our God,
> the Sacrament of thy will,
> has been fulfilled and completed,
> for we have had the memory of thy death,
> we have seen the image of thy resurrection,
> we have been filled with thine eternal life,
> we have enjoyed this immortal food,
> which grant us also in the age to come.

(Final prayer of Liturgy of St. Basil.)